UK TOP 1000 SINGLES

Paul Gambaccini, Tim Rice, Jo Rice

Editorial Associate: Tony Brown

GUINNESS BOOKS

Picture acknowledgements: London Features International;
Keystone Collection; BBC Hulton Picture Library; Syndication
International.

Editor: Honor Head
Designer: Alan Hamp
Picture Editor: Alex Goldberg

Published in Great Britain by Guinness Publishing Ltd,
33 London Road, Enfield, Middlesex

Typeset by Ace Filmsetting Ltd, Frome, Somerset
Printed and bound in Great Britain by The Bath Press, Bath

British Library Cataloguing in Publication Data
Gambaccini, Paul
  Guinness UK top 1000 singles.
  1. Pop music. Sound discs. British top
  forty singles, 1952 to 1987. Discographies
  I. Title II. Rice, Tim III. Rice, Jo
  016.7899'1245

  ISBN 0-85112-889-0

Contents

Introduction

This one's for fun. After studying the British record charts for years, we couldn't refuse our publishers' offer to compile a chart of our own. Guinness suggested we prepare a British version of the US hit singles list printed by the pioneering American chartologist Joel Whitburn. We had long recommended the purchase of his books and already enjoyed his *USA Top 1000 Singles*.

The proposal was attractive. Who wouldn't want to know what the biggest hits of all-time are, in order? When it comes strictly to chart performance, do any of Ken Dodd's records rate higher than all of Rod Stewart's? Are Frankie Goes to Hollywood bigger than Gerry and the Pacemakers after all? Where do our personal favourites figure?

We made an early and limited attempt to compile the biggest UK chart hits in *British Hit Singles* (Third Edition), published in 1981. We now go into much greater depth using a system similar but not identical to Whitburn's American methodology. It is far simpler than that used in *Hit Singles 3*. Some readers of that book suggested we concentrate on performance at the top of the chart rather than use a points system that rewards longevity, since records can remain in the lower reaches of the survey with few sales. We have taken the recommendation to heart.

In this book we rate the hits according to weeks spent at number one. When a tie occurs we compare weeks at number two. If there is still a tie we refer to weeks at three and so forth down the chart until all ties are broken. After we have ordered all the number ones we go on to the singles that peaked at two. There have been more than enough of these to fill the top 1000. It will interest many readers to know that the lowest point we had to look to in order to break a tie was 26.

In the pages herein we list our top 1000 of the rock era. Next to a title we give the number of weeks the disc spent at each of the top three positions. When these figures are the same, be assured that the tie was broken by reference to a lower position. No two records in our top 1000 had identical chart histories.

We begin our computations with *Rock Around The Clock*, the first rock 'n' roll number one, even though the British charts began in 1952. Prior to Bill Haley's hit, singles moved much more slowly up and down the top ten, and to include these early successes would incline the top 1000 in favour of the early and mid-Fifties. *I Believe* (Frankie Laine), *Rose Marie* (Slim Whitman) and *Cara Mia* (David Whitfield) would finish as the top three of pop history. For such a short era to dominate the all-time totals would be inequitable, so we have omitted the pre-rock chart period from November 1952 to November 1955. With a tip of the hat to artists who achieved at that time we acknowledge that, in chart terms, this three yea period was an era unto itself. The charts we have consulted for our listing are the same we use for *Hit Singles*: the *New Musical Express* until the end of February 1960 and *Record Retailer* (which became *Music Week*) from the beginning of March of that year.

When looking at our top 1000 please remember that this is not a sales chart. Although the weekly chart always ranks singles in order of sales, the total volume of purchase changes every week and is subject to seasonal fluctuations. A number one record on chart will most likely sell different amount of copies than the leader the weeks before and after. Merely comparing charts cannot provide clues to total sales. Indeed, it is almost certainly impossible to compile an accurate top 1000 based on sales, since many labels no longer exist and some that still do either did not keep strictly precise figures or are reluctant to release them.

So here it is, our ranking of the biggest UK hits of the rock era based on highest chart positions reached and sustained. Can you guess the number one? If you brilliantly manage to identify that champion, can you make a successful surmise as to the identity of number 1000?

We hope you get as much enjoyment as we did from seeing the surprises. As we said, this one's for fun. In 1989 we'll be back in business with *Hit Singles 7*. We'll see you then for our biennial feast of facts and photos. Until then, don't tell The Sex Pistols they just missed the top 1000 with number 1001.

Paul Gambaccini
Tim Rice
Jo Rice

THE RANKING

A listing of the Top 1000 hits,
in rank order, from 1955–1987.

John Travolta and Olivia Newton-John

Year	Weeks on Chart	Weeks at No 1	No 2	No 3	Rank	Title Artist
78	26	9	3	0	1	**You're The One That I Want** John Travolta and Olivia Newton-John
77	17	9	1	0	2	**Mull Of Kintyre/Girls' School** Wings
57	25	9	0	1	3	**Diana** Paul Anka
84	21	9	0	1	4	**Two Tribes** Frankie Goes To Hollywood
75	17	9	0	1	5	**Bohemian Rhapsody** Queen
58	17	8	2	1	6	**Magic Moments** Perry Como
62	19	8	1	1	7	**Wonderful Land** Shadows
60	21	8	1	0	8	**It's Now Or Never** Elvis Presley
69	26	8	0	3	9	**Sugar Sugar** Archies
57	18	7	3	2	10	**Young Love** Tab Hunter
58	21	7	3	1	11	**All I Have To Do Is Dream/Claudette** Everly Brothers
62	28	7	3	0	12	**I Remember You** Frank Ifield
56	19	7	2	1	13	**Just Walkin' In The Rain** Johnnie Ray
66	22	7	1	1	14	**Green Green Grass Of Home** Tom Jones
63	25	7	1	1	15	**From Me To You** Beatles
57	27	7	1	1	16	**All Shook Up** Elvis Presley
60	18	7	0	1	17	**Cathy's Clown** Everly Brothers
78	19	7	0	1	18	**Summer Nights** John Travolta and Olivia Newton-John
57	12	7	0	1	19	**Mary's Boy Child** Harry Belafonte
70	20	7	0	0	20	**In The Summertime** Mungo Jerry
67	13	7	0	0	21	**Hello Goodbye** Beatles
63	27	6	6	6	22	**She Loves You** Beatles
56	22	6	4	1	23	**Whatever Will Be Will Be** Doris Day
59	23	6	3	2	24	**Living Doll** Cliff Richard and the Drifters
59	25	6	3	2	25	**What Do You Want To Make Those Eyes At Me For** Emile Ford & The Checkmates
62	21	6	3	0	26	**The Young Ones** Cliff Richard and the Shadows
58	25	6	2	1	27	**Who's Sorry Now** Connie Francis
84	26	6	2	1	28	**I Just Called To Say I Love You** Stevie Wonder
69	25	6	2	1	29	**Two Little Boys** Rolf Harris
58	19	6	2	0	30	**Carolina Moon/Stupid Cupid** Connie Francis
67	56	6	2	0	31	**Release Me** Engelbert Humperdinck
76	16	6	2	0	32	**Save Your Kisses For Me** Brotherhood Of Man
68	21	6	2	0	33	**Those Were The Days** Mary Hopkin
70	14	6	2	0	34	**I Hear You Knockin'** Dave Edmunds
70	22	6	1	1	35	**The Wonder Of You** Elvis Presley
76	14	6	1	1	36	**Don't Go Breaking My Heart** Elton John and Kiki Dee
61	28	6	1	0	37	**Wooden Heart** Elvis Presley

Bay City Rollers

Year	Weeks on Chart	No 1	No 2	No 3	Rank	Title Artist
69	22	6	1	0	38	**Get Back** Beatles with Billy Preston
75	16	6	1	0	39	**Bye Bye Baby** Bay City Rollers
71	17	6	1	0	40	**Hot Love** T. Rex
...	.....	...	...	...		
76	15	6	1	0	41	**Dancing Queen** Abba
70	19	6	0	1	42	**Band Of Gold** Freda Payne
83	20	6	0	1	43	**Karma Chameleon** Culture Club
79	19	6	0	1	44	**Bright Eyes** Art Garfunkel
56	14	6	0	0	45	**No Other Love** Ronnie Hilton
67	28	6	0	0	46	**A Whiter Shade Of Pale** Procul Harum
84	15	6	0	0	47	**Hello** Lionel Richie
83	48	5	4	5	48	**Relax!** Frankie Goes To Hollywood
55	57	5	4	1	49	**Rock Around The Clock** Bill Haley and His Comets
78	40	5	3	3	50	**Rivers Of Babylon/Brown Girl In The Ring** Boney M
...	.....	...	...	...		
56	24	5	3	1	51	**I'll Be Home** Pat Boone
59	15	5	3	0	52	**A Fool Such As I/I Need Your Love Tonight** Elvis Presley
72	20	5	2	2	53	**Without You** Nilsson
65	24	5	2	1	54	**Tears** Ken Dodd
71	26	5	2	1	55	**Maggie May** Rod Stewart
58	15	5	2	1	56	**It's Only Make Believe** Conway Twitty
60	21	5	2	1	57	**Apache** Shadows
71	27	5	2	1	58	**Knock Three Times** Dawn
71	34	5	2	1	59	**Chirpy Chirpy Cheep Cheep** Middle Of The Road
85	34	5	2	0	60	**The Power Of Love** Jennifer Rush
...	.....	...	...	...		
65	12	5	2	0	61	**Day Tripper/We Can Work It Out** Beatles
77	13	5	2	0	62	**Knowing Me Knowing You** Abba
58	18	5	1	4	63	**When** Kalin Twins
67	27	5	1	3	64	**The Last Waltz** Engelbert Humperdinck
62	17	5	1	2	65	**Lovesick Blues** Frank Ifield
62	17	5	1	2	66	**Good Luck Charm** Elvis Presley
84	20	5	1	2	67	**Do They Know It's Christmas** Band Aid
59	17	5	1	2	68	**Travellin' Light** Cliff Richard and the Shadows
72	27	5	1	2	69	**Amazing Grace** The Pipes and Drums and Military Band of the Royal Scots Dragoon Guards
69	17	5	1	2	70	**Honky Tonk Women** Rolling Stones
...	.....	...	...	...		
66	25	5	1	1	71	**Distant Drums** Jim Reeves
87	18	5	1	1	72	**Never Gonna Give You Up** Rick Astley
73	15	5	1	1	73	**Blockbuster** Sweet
71	17	5	1	1	74	**My Sweet Lord** George Harrison

Year	Weeks on Chart	Weeks at No 1	No 2	No 3	Rank	Title Artist
63	24	5	1	1	75	**I Want To Hold Your Hand** Beatles
88	16	5	1	1	76	**I Should Be So Lucky** Kylie Minogue
72	24	5	1	0	77	**Long Haired Lover From Liverpool** Little Jimmy Osmond
77	13	5	1	0	78	**Way Down** Elvis Presley
78	14	5	1	0	79	**Three Times A Lady** Commodores
81	13	5	1	0	80	**Don't You Want Me** Human League
...	.....	...	...	...		
79	12	5	1	0	81	**Another Brick In The Wall (Part II)** Pink Floyd
64	14	5	1	0	82	**I Feel Fine** Beatles
62	25	5	0	2	83	**Telstar** Tornados
72	23	5	0	1	84	**Puppy Love** Donny Osmond
85	16	5	0	1	85	**19** Paul Hardcastle
83	17	5	0	1	86	**Uptown Girl** Billy Joel
73	31	5	0	1	87	**Merry Xmas Everybody** Slade
57	12	5	0	0	88	**Cumberland Gap** Lonnie Donegan
70	12	5	0	0	89	**Love Grows (Where My Rosemary Goes)** Edison Lighthouse
87	15	5	0	0	90	**China In Your Hand** T'Pau
...	.....	...	...	...		
81	15	5	0	0	91	**Stand And Deliver** Adam and the Ants
83	11	5	0	0	92	**Only You** Flying Pickets
59	20	4	4	2	93	**Dream Lover** Bobby Darin
56	21	4	4	2	94	**A Woman In Love** Frankie Laine
75	31	4	3	2	95	**Sailing** Rod Stewart
73	14	4	3	1	96	**I Love You Love Me Love** Gary Glitter
76	15	4	3	0	97	**Fernando** Abba
61	15	4	3	0	98	**Johnny Remember Me** John Leyton
59	15	4	3	0	99	**Only Sixteen** Craig Douglas
60	17	4	3	0	100	**Why** Anthony Newley
...	.....	...	...	...		
72	17	4	3	0	101	**My Ding-A-Ling** Chuck Berry
79	14	4	3	0	102	**We Don't Talk Anymore** Cliff Richard
58	19	4	2	2	103	**As I Love You** Shirley Bassey
71	17	4	2	2	104	**Ernie (The Fastest Milkman In The West)** Benny Hill
76	22	4	2	1	105	**Mississippi** Pussycat
56	14	4	2	1	106	**Lay Down Your Arms** Anne Shelton
57	13	4	2	1	107	**Garden Of Eden** Frankie Vaughan
68	30	4	2	1	108	**Young Girl** Union Gap featuring Gary Puckett
85	16	4	2	1	109	**I Know Him So Well** Elaine Paige and Barbara Dickson
82	17	4	2	1	110	**Come On Eileen** Dexys Midnight Runners
...	.....	...	...	...		
68	24	4	2	0	111	**Lily The Pink** Scaffold
77	13	4	2	0	112	**I Don't Want To Talk About It/First Cut Is The Deepest** Rod Stewart

Kylie Minogue

Year	Weeks on Chart	Weeks at No 1	No 2	No 3	Rank	Title Artist
82	15	4	2	0	113	**Eye Of The Tiger** Survivor
67	17	4	2	0	114	**Massachusetts** Bee Gees
63	19	4	2	0	115	**You'll Never Walk Alone** Gerry and the Pacemakers
85	16	4	2	0	116	**Frankie** Sister Sledge
56	11	4	2	0	117	**Sixteen Tons** Tennessee Ernie Ford
57	31	4	2	0	118	**Reet Petite** Jackie Wilson
63	15	4	2	0	119	**I Like It** Gerry and the Pacemakers
72	22	4	2	0	120	**Eye Level** Simon Park Orchestra
79	23	4	2	0	121	**Are 'Friends' Electric** Tubeway Army
69	16	4	2	0	122	**Where Do You Go To My Lovely** Peter Sarstedt
79	12	4	2	0	123	**I Don't Like Mondays** Boomtown Rats
59	30	4	1	3	124	**Side Saddle** Russ Conway
67	17	4	1	3	125	**San Francisco (Be Sure To Wear Flowers In Your Hair)** Scott McKenzie
62	20	4	1	2	126	**Rock-A-Hula Baby/Can't Help Falling In Love** Elvis Presley
73	40	4	1	2	127	**Tie A Yellow Ribbon Round The Old Oak Tree** Dawn
87	17	4	1	2	128	**Nothing's Gonna Stop Us Now** Starship
68	25	4	1	2	129	**The Good The Bad And The Ugly** Hugo Montenegro
76	16	4	1	3	130	**Don't Give Up On Us** David Soul
68	29	4	1	1	131	**What A Wonderful World/Cabaret** Louis Armstrong
67	17	4	1	1	132	**I'm A Believer** Monkees
72	19	4	1	1	133	**Mouldy Old Dough** Lieutenant Pigeon
86	14	4	1	1	134	**Don't Leave Me This Way** Communards with Sarah Jane Morris
73	12	4	1	1	135	**I'm The Leader Of The Gang (I Am)** Gary Glitter
61	23	4	1	1	136	**Are You Lonesome Tonight** Elvis Presley
71	18	4	1	1	137	**I'm Still Waiting** Diana Ross
85	12	4	1	1	138	**Easy Lover** Philip Bailey (duet with Phil Collins)
71	21	4	1	0	139	**I'd Like To Teach The World To Sing** New Seekers
85	14	4	1	0	140	**Into The Groove** Madonna
61	13	4	1	0	141	**Little Sister/His Latest Flame** Elvis Presley
72	14	4	1	0	142	**Metal Guru** T. Rex
87	11	4	1	0	143	**Always On My Mind** Pet Shop Boys
81	12	4	1	0	144	**Prince Charming** Adam and the Ants
86	13	4	1	0	145	**When The Going Gets Tough The Tough Get Going** Billy Ocean

Year	Weeks on Chart	Weeks at No 1	No 2	No 3	Rank	Title Artist
86	10	4	1	0	146	**Take My Breath Away (love theme from *Top Gun*)** Berlin
60	13	4	1	0	147	**My Old Man's A Dustman** Lonnie Donegan
74	14	4	1	0	148	**She** Charles Aznavour
79	12	4	1	0	149	**Heart Of Glass** Blondie
61	15	4	1	0	150	**Surrender** Elvis Presley
74	11	4	1	0	151	**Tiger Feet** Mud
74	10	4	1	0	152	**Sugar Baby Love** Rubettes
78	8	4	1	0	153	**Mary's Boy Child-Oh My Lord** Boney M
83	11	4	1	0	154	**Every Breath You Take** Police
66	11	4	1	0	155	**The Sun Ain't Gonna Shine Anymore** Walker Brothers
73	12	4	1	0	156	**Cum On Feel The Noize** Slade
83	12	4	1	0	157	**True** Spandau Ballet
71	15	4	0	3	158	**Coz I Luv You** Slade
56	16	4	0	2	159	**Memories Are Made Of This** Dean Martin
82	16	4	0	2	160	**Save Your Love** Renée and Renato
77	21	4	0	2	161	**I Feel Love** Donna Summer
74	12	4	0	2	162	**Seasons In The Sun** Terry Jacks
71	13	4	0	1	163	**Get It On** T. Rex
79	15	4	0	1	164	**I Will Survive** Gloria Gaynor
84	14	4	0	1	165	**The Reflex** Duran Duran
73	17	4	0	1	166	**See My Baby Jive** Wizzard
64	17	4	0	1	167	**You're My World** Cilla Black
66	13	4	0	1	168	**Yellow Submarine/Eleanor Rigby** Beatles
78	13	4	0	1	169	**Wuthering Heights** Kate Bush
87	15	4	0	1	170	**You Win Again** Bee Gees
85	12	4	0	1	171	**Dancing In The Street** David Bowie and Mick Jagger
80	14	4	0	1	172	**Don't Stand So Close To Me** Police
77	12	4	0	0	173	**The Name Of The Game** Abba
75	24	4	0	0	174	**Imagine** John Lennon
74	13	4	0	0	175	**Lonely This Christmas** Mud
81	12	4	0	0	176	**Green Door** Shakin' Stevens
66	14	4	0	0	177	**These Boots Are Made For Walkin'** Nancy Sinatra
81	13	4	0	0	178	**It's My Party** Dave Stewart with Barbara Gaskin
73	10	4	0	0	179	**Young Love** Donny Osmond
59	21	3	5	3	180	**It Doesn't Matter Anymore** Buddy Holly
58	17	3	5	2	181	**Hoots Mon** Lord Rockingham's XI
61	22	3	5	1	182	**Runaway** Del Shannon

Year	Weeks on Chart	Weeks at No 1	No 2	No 3	Rank	Title Artist
62	18	3	5	0	183	**The Next Time/Bachelor Boy** Cliff Richard and the Shadows
56	22	3	4	2	184	**Singing The Blues** Guy Mitchell
56	16	3	4	2	185	**Poor People Of Paris** Winifred Atwell
60	18	3	4	1	186	**Please Don't Tease** Cliff Richard and the Shadows
76	15	3	4	1	187	**Under The Moon Of Love** Showaddywaddy
56	16	3	4	1	188	**Why Do Fools Fall In Love** Teenagers featuring Frankie Lymon
78	16	3	4	0	189	**Y.M.C.A.** Village People
59	23	3	4	0	190	**What Do You Want** Adam Faith
56	18	3	3	6	191	**It's Almost Tomorrow** Dreamweavers
61	23	3	3	3	192	**You Don't Know** Helen Shapiro
61	19	3	3	1	193	**Walkin' Back To Happiness** Helen Shapiro
58	15	3	3	1	194	**Whole Lotta Woman** Marvin Rainwater
84	17	3	3	1	195	**Careless Whisper** George Michael
62	17	3	3	1	196	**Return To Sender** Elvis Presley
67	16	3	3	1	197	**All You Need Is Love** Beatles
64	18	3	3	0	198	**Oh Pretty Woman** Roy Orbison
63	18	3	3	0	199	**How Do You Do It** Gerry and the Pacemakers
75	12	3	3	0	200	**Whispering Grass** Windsor Davies and Don Estelle
60	15	3	3	0	201	**Good Timin'** Jimmy Jones
78	10	3	3	0	202	**Take A Chance On Me** Abba
70	20	3	2	2	203	**Bridge Over Troubled Water** Simon and Garfunkel
71	17	3	2	2	204	**Hey Girl Don't Bother Me** Tams
70	17	3	2	2	205	**Back Home** England World Cup Squad
65	17	3	2	1	206	**The Carnival Is Over** Seekers
76	16	3	2	1	207	**If You Leave Me Now** Chicago
82	16	3	2	1	208	**Fame** Irene Cara
79	17	3	2	1	209	**When You're In Love With A Beautiful Woman** Dr. Hook
69	15	3	2	1	210	**I Heard It Through The Grapevine** Marvin Gaye
64	15	3	2	1	211	**A Hard Day's Night** Beatles
66	20	3	2	1	212	**Strangers In The Night** Frank Sinatra
74	17	3	2	1	213	**Gonna Make You A Star** David Essex
81	17	3	2	1	214	**This Ole House** Shakin' Stevens
86	14	3	2	1	215	**Papa Don't Preach** Madonna
83	14	3	2	1	216	**Red Red Wine** UB 40
69	15	3	2	1	217	**Bad Moon Rising** Creedence Clearwater Revival

Spandau Ballet

Year	Weeks on Chart	Weeks at No 1	No 2	No 3	Rank	Title Artist
86	14	3	2	1	218	**The Lady In Red** Chris De Burgh
83	15	3	2	1	219	**Wherever I Lay My Hat (That's My Home)** Paul Young
70	23	3	2	0	220	**Wand'rin' Star** Lee Marvin
70	28	3	2	0	221	**Grandad** Clive Dunn
68	18	3	2	0	222	**Mony Mony** Tommy James and the Shondells
68	13	3	2	0	223	**Cinderella Rockefella** Esther and Abi Ofarim
86	17	3	2	0	224	**Chain Reaction** Diana Ross
65	17	3	2	0	225	**Help!** Beatles
86	15	3	2	0	226	**I Want To Wake Up With You** Boris Gardiner
81	14	3	2	0	227	**Ghost Town** Specials
84	16	3	2	0	228	**I Feel For You** Chaka Khan
61	13	3	2	0	229	**Tower Of Strength** Frankie Vaughan
82	15	3	2	0	230	**The Lion Sleeps Tonight** Tight Fit
63	18	3	2	0	231	**Summer Holiday** Cliff Richard and the Shadows
83	12	3	2	0	232	**Down Under** Men At Work
75	10	3	2	0	233	**Hold Me Close** David Essex
74	14	3	2	0	234	**Billy Don't Be A Hero** Paper Lace
76	12	3	2	0	235	**When A Child Is Born (Soleado)** Johnny Mathis
84	12	3	2	0	236	**99 Red Balloons** Nena
58	31	3	1	4	237	**Jailhouse Rock** Elvis Presley
57	16	3	1	3	238	**Yes Tonight Josephine** Johnnie Ray
61	16	3	1	2	239	**Walk Right Back/Ebony Eyes** Everly Brothers
67	18	3	1	2	240	**Puppet On A String** Sandie Shaw
78	19	3	1	2	241	**Matchstalk Men And Matchstalk Cats And Dogs** Brian and Michael
77	14	3	1	2	242	**Silver Lady** David Soul
57	15	3	1	2	243	**That'll Be The Day** Crickets
76	15	3	1	2	244	**I Love To Love (But My Baby Loves To Dance)** Tina Charles
75	11	3	1	2	245	**I Can't Give You Anything (But My Love)** Stylistics
58	17	3	1	1	246	**It's All In The Game** Tommy Edwards
77	11	3	1	1	247	**So You Win Again** Hot Chocolate
74	14	3	1	1	248	**Rock Your Baby** George McCrae
60	16	3	1	1	249	**Tell Laura I Love Her** Ricky Valance
59	12	3	1	1	250	**One Night/I Got Stung** Elvis Presley
66	16	3	1	1	251	**Reach Out I'll Be There** Four Tops
82	18	3	1	1	252	**Do You Really Want To Hurt Me** Culture Club

Chris De Burgh

Year	Weeks on Chart	Weeks at No 1	No 2	No 3	Rank	Title Artist
84	14	3	1	1	253	**Freedom** Wham!
64	17	3	1	1	254	**Anyone Who Had A Heart** Cilla Black
72	13	3	1	1	255	**Son Of My Father** Chicory Tip
63	14	3	1	1	256	**Do You Love Me** Brian Poole and the Tremeloes
77	13	3	1	1	257	**When I Need You** Leo Sayer
75	12	3	1	1	258	**Stand By Your Man** Tammy Wynette
88	13	3	1	1	259	**I Think We're Alone Now** Tiffany
74	12	3	1	1	260	**Everything I Own** Ken Boothe
80	16	3	1	1	261	**Woman In Love** Barbra Streisand
83	14	3	1	1	262	**Baby Jane** Rod Stewart
72	12	3	1	1	263	**School's Out** Alice Cooper
65	14	3	1	1	264	**Ticket To Ride** Beatles
72	10	3	1	1	265	**Mama Weer All Crazee Now** Slade
73	15	3	1	1	266	**Daydreamer/The Puppy Song** David Cassidy
82	10	3	1	1	267	**Ebony And Ivory** Paul McCartney with Stevie Wonder
67	15	3	1	0	268	**Silence Is Golden** Tremeloes
65	14	3	1	0	269	**I'm Alive** Hollies
80	14	3	1	0	270	**Crying** Don McLean
74	13	3	1	0	271	**Kung Fu Fighting** Carl Douglas
86	11	3	1	0	272	**Living Doll** Cliff Richard and the Young Ones
80	12	3	1	0	273	**Super Trouper** Abba
81	12	3	1	0	274	**Making Your Mind Up** Bucks Fizz
87	11	3	1	0	275	**It's A Sin** Pet Shop Boys
83	14	3	1	0	276	**Give It Up** K.C. and the Sunshine Band
86	10	3	1	0	277	**A Different Corner** George Michael
80	12	3	1	0	278	**Theme From M*A*S*H (Suicide Is Painless)** Mash
64	17	3	1	0	279	**Can't Buy Me Love** Beatles
63	13	3	1	0	280	**Wayward Wind** Frank Ifield
79	13	3	1	0	281	**Sunday Girl** Blondie
75	9	3	1	0	282	**Give A Little Love** Bay City Rollers
86	13	3	1	0	283	**Every Loser Wins** Nick Berry
82	15	3	1	0	284	**I Don't Wanna Dance** Eddy Grant
82	12	3	1	0	285	**Seven Tears** Goombay Dance Band
55	7	3	1	0	286	**Christmas Alphabet** Dickie Valentine
70	18	3	1	0	287	**Woodstock** Matthews Southern Comfort
66	12	3	1	0	288	**Pretty Flamingo** Manfred Mann
74	9	3	1	0	289	**Love Me For A Reason** Osmonds
76	23	3	1	0	290	**You To Me Are Everything** Real Thing
79	18	3	1	0	291	**One Day At A Time** Lena Martell
62	14	3	1	0	292	**She's Not You** Elvis Presley

Tiffany

Police

Year	Weeks on Chart	No 1	No 2	No 3	Rank	Title Artist
83	14	3	1	0	293	**Let's Dance** David Bowie
82	13	3	1	0	294	**Pass The Dutchie** Musical Youth
65	13	3	1	0	295	**The Last Time** Rolling Stones
61	11	3	1	0	296	**Stand By Me** Ben E. King
64	11	3	1	0	297	**(There's) Always Something There To Remind Me** Sandie Shaw
79	11	3	1	0	298	**Message In A Bottle** Police
75	10	3	1	0	299	**January** Pilot
63	14	3	0	3	300	**Bad To Me** Billy J. Kramer and the Dakotas
64	15	3	0	2	301	**Needles And Pins** Searchers
69	14	3	0	2	302	**Ballad Of John And Yoko** Beatles
77	13	3	0	2	303	**Chanson D'Amour** Manhattan Transfer
69	13	3	0	2	304	**In The Year 2525 (Exordium And Terminus)** Zager and Evans
68	18	3	0	2	305	**Baby Come Back** Equals
81	10	3	0	2	306	**Shaddup You Face** Joe Dolce Music Theatre
63	13	3	0	1	307	**Diamonds** Jet Harris and Tony Meehan
84	16	3	0	1	308	**I Want To Know What Love Is** Foreigner
86	15	3	0	1	309	**Spirit In The Sky** Doctor and the Medics
68	20	3	0	1	310	**Ob-La-Di Ob-La-Da** Marmalade
65	12	3	0	1	311	**Get Off Of My Cloud** Rolling Stones
69	12	3	0	1	312	**Something In The Air** Thunderclap Newman
80	15	3	0	1	313	**Going Underground/Dreams Of Children** Jam
65	14	3	0	1	314	**Long Live Love** Sandie Shaw
86	11	3	0	1	315	**The Chicken Song** Spitting Image
82	9	3	0	1	316	**A Town Called Malice/Precious** Jam
73	10	3	0	0	317	**Skweeze Me Pleeze Me** Slade
87	7	3	0	1	318	**Let It Be** Ferry Aid
66	10	3	0	0	319	**Michelle** Overlanders
58	15	2	6	1	320	**The Story Of My Life** Michael Holliday
57	19	2	5	0	321	**Gamblin' Man/Putting On The Style** Lonnie Donegan
59	19	2	4	2	322	**Mack The Knife** Bobby Darin
63	16	2	4	1	323	**Confessin'** Frank Ifield
78	20	2	4	1	324	**Night Fever** Bee Gees
67	18	2	4	0	325	**Somethin' Stupid** Nancy Sinatra and Frank Sinatra
85	16	2	4	0	326	**Saving All My Love For You** Whitney Houston
68	23	2	3	1	327	**Hey Jude** Beatles
57	16	2	3	1	328	**Butterfly** Andy Williams
63	19	2	3	0	329	**Glad All Over** Dave Clark Five

Phil Collins

Year	Weeks on Chart	Weeks at No 1	Weeks at No 2	Weeks at No 3	Rank	Title Artist
60	16	2	3	0	330	**I Love You** Cliff Richard and the Shadows
64	18	2	3	0	331	**It's Over** Roy Orbison
70	20	2	3	0	332	**Spirit In The Sky** Norman Greenbaum
87	16	2	3	0	333	**I Wanna Dance With Somebody (Who Loves Me)** Whitney Houston
65	15	2	3	0	334	**Crying In The Chapel** Elvis Presley
82	11	2	3	0	335	**Goody Two Shoes** Adam Ant
81	36	2	3	0	336	**Tainted Love** Soft Cell
60	24	2	2	2	337	**Only The Lonely** Roy Orbison
62	17	2	2	2	338	**I Can't Stop Loving You** Ray Charles
60	15	2	2	2	339	**Three Steps To Heaven** Eddie Cochran
64	15	2	2	2	340	**Have I The Right** Honeycombs
58	17	2	2	1	341	**On The Street Where You Live** Vic Damone
62	19	2	2	1	342	**Come Outside** Mike Sarne with Wendy Richard
74	16	2	2	1	343	**When Will I See You Again** Three Degrees
64	13	2	2	1	344	**Little Children** Billy J. Kramer and the Dakotas
68	12	2	2	1	345	**Everlasting Love** Love Affair
75	11	2	2	1	346	**I Only Have Eyes For You** Art Garfunkel
61	19	2	2	1	347	**Moon River** Danny Williams
78	15	2	2	1	348	**Rat Trap** Boomtown Rats
64	15	2	2	1	349	**I'm Into Something Good** Herman's Hermits
87	14	2	2	1	350	**Heaven Is A Place On Earth** Belinda Carlisle
70	16	2	2	1	351	**All Kinds Of Everything** Dana
81	14	2	2	1	352	**One Day In Your Life** Michael Jackson
82	16	2	2	1	353	**You Can't Hurry Love** Phil Collins
87	14	2	2	1	354	**Pump Up The Volume/Anitina (The First Time I See She Dance)** M/A/R/R/S
68	11	2	2	1	355	**The Mighty Quinn** Manfred Mann
76	10	2	2	1	356	**December '63 (Oh What A Night)** Four Seasons
85	13	2	2	1	357	**Total Eclipse Of The Heart** Bonnie Tyler
80	12	2	2	1	358	**Use It Up And Wear It Out** Odyssey
76	13	2	2	1	359	**Combine Harvester (Brand New Key)** Wurzels
72	14	2	2	1	360	**Telegram Sam** T. Rex
59	19	2	2	0	361	**Roulette** Russ Conway
65	12	2	2	0	362	**I Got You Babe** Sonny and Cher
67	16	2	2	0	363	**Baby Now That I've Found You** Foundations

Year	Weeks on Chart	No 1	No 2	No 3	Rank	Title Artist
81	16	2	2	0	364	**The Land Of Make Believe** Bucks Fizz
69	24	2	2	0	365	**Space Oddity** David Bowie
68	11	2	2	0	366	**Do Wah Diddy Diddy** Manfred Mann
65	23	2	2	0	367	**I'll Never Find Another You** Seekers
84	16	2	2	0	368	**Wake Me Up Before You Go-Go** Wham!
60	15	2	2	0	369	**Running Bear** Johnny Preston
85	12	2	2	0	370	**I'm Your Man** Wham!
75	9	2	2	0	371	**If** Telly Savalas
72	15	2	2	0	372	**Vincent** Don McLean
66	20	2	2	0	373	**Good Vibrations** Beach Boys
85	12	2	2	0	374	**The Sun Always Shines On T.V.** a-ha
80	12	2	2	0	375	**The Tide Is High** Blondie
80	14	2	2	0	376	**Geno** Dexy's Midnight Runners
86	10	2	2	0	377	**The Edge Of Heaven/Where Did Your Heart Go** Wham!
87	9	2	2	0	378	**I Knew You Were Waiting (For Me)** Aretha Franklin and George Michael
80	12	2	2	0	379	**Coward Of The County** Kenny Rogers
74	11	2	2	0	380	**Devil Gate Drive** Suzi Quatro
74	9	2	2	0	381	**Waterloo** Abba
80	11	2	2	0	382	**There's No One Quite Like Grandma** St Winifred's School Choir
66	11	2	2	0	383	**Paperback Writer** Beatles
69	16	2	2	0	384	**(If Paradise Is) Half As Nice** Amen Corner
86	15	2	1	3	385	**The Final Countdown** Europe
60	17	2	1	3	386	**Poetry In Motion** Johnny Tillotson
63	16	2	1	3	387	**Sweets For My Sweet** Searchers
81	11	2	1	2	388	**Woman** John Lennon
87	9	2	1	2	389	**La Isla Bonita** Madonna
66	12	2	1	2	390	**With A Girl Like You** Troggs
75	14	2	1	2	391	**Mamma Mia** Abba
65	12	2	1	2	392	**(I Can't Get No) Satisfaction** Rolling Stones
74	14	2	1	1	393	**You're The First The Last My Everything** Barry White
68	11	2	1	1	394	**Jumping Jack Flash** Rolling Stones
71	15	2	1	1	395	**Double Barrel** Dave and Ansil Collins
77	10	2	1	1	396	**Free** Deniece Williams
80	10	2	1	1	397	**Ashes To Ashes** David Bowie
65	14	2	1	1	398	**Mr. Tambourine Man** Byrds
75	11	2	1	1	399	**I'm Not In Love** 10 C.C.
72	11	2	1	1	400	**How Can I Be Sure** David Cassidy
79	11	2	1	1	401	**Ring My Bell** Anita Ward
80	11	2	1	1	402	**Xanadu** Olivia Newton-John and the Electric Light Orchestra

Madonna

Year	Weeks on Chart	Weeks at No 1	No 2	No 3	Rank	Title Artist
64	11	2	1	1	403	**Don't Throw Your Love Away** Searchers
66	13	2	1	1	404	**Sunny Afternoon** Kinks
83	13	2	1	1	405	**Too Shy** Kajagoogoo
81	13	2	1	1	406	**Being With You** Smokey Robinson
61	13	2	1	1	407	**Blue Moon** Marcels
79	17	2	1	1	408	**Brass In Pocket** Pretenders
72	14	2	1	1	409	**Clair** Gilbert O'Sullivan
79	10	2	1	1	410	**Tragedy** Bee Gees
...	....	..	...	...		
67	13	2	1	1	411	**Let The Heartaches Begin** Long John Baldry
68	13	2	1	1	412	**Congratulations** Cliff Richard
75	9	2	1	1	413	**Oh Boy** Mud
80	9	2	1	1	414	**Atomic** Blondie
87	9	2	1	1	415	**Jack Your Body** Steve 'Silk' Hurley
75	9	2	1	1	416	**Make Me Smile (Come Up And See Me)** Steve Harley and Cockney Rebel
66	10	2	1	1	417	**Somebody Help Me** Spencer Davis Group
87	12	2	1	1	418	**Star Trekkin'** Firm
80	8	2	1	1	419	**What's Another Year** Johnny Logan
85	11	2	1	1	420	**Merry Christmas Everyone** Shakin' Stevens
...	....	..	...	...		
83	9	2	1	1	421	**Is There Something I Should Know** Duran Duran
64	11	2	1	0	422	**A World Without Love** Peter and Gordon
85	16	2	1	0	423	**A Good Heart** Feargal Sharkey
71	13	2	1	0	424	**Baby Jump** Mungo Jerry
64	16	2	1	0	425	**You Really Got Me** Kinks
80	10	2	1	0	426	**The Winner Takes It All** Abba
64	12	2	1	0	427	**Yeh Yeh** Georgie Fame and the Blue Flames
80	10	2	1	0	428	**Too Much Too Young (EP)** Specials AKA featuring Rico
84	23	2	1	0	429	**You Spin Me Round (Like a Record)** Dead Or Alive
87	11	2	1	0	430	**La Bamba** Los Lobos
...	....	..	..	...		
85	9	2	1	0	431	**We Are The World** USA For Africa
82	9	2	1	0	432	**House Of Fun** Madness
87	9	2	1	0	433	**Everything I Own** Boy George
83	12	2	1	0	434	**Pipes Of Peace** Paul McCartney
81	11	2	1	0	435	**Under Pressure** Queen and David Bowie
82	9	2	1	0	436	**Beat Surrender** Jam
67	14	2	0	3	437	**This Is My Song** Petula Clark
73	13	2	0	3	438	**Get Down** Gilbert O'Sullivan
61	15	2	0	2	439	**Temptation** Everly Brothers
85	15	2	0	2	440	**West End Girls** Pet Shop Boys
...	....	..	...	...		

Petula Clark

Year	Weeks on Chart	Weeks at No 1	No 2	No 3	Rank	Title Artist
65	25	2	0	2	441	**You've Lost That Lovin' Feeling** Righteous Brothers
80	14	2	0	2	442	**Working My Way Back To You–Forgive Me Girl** Detroit Spinners
81	11	2	0	2	443	**Jealous Guy** Roxy Music
80	16	2	0	1	444	**Feels Like I'm In Love** Kelly Marie
63	19	2	0	1	445	**You'll Never Walk Alone** Crowd
64	15	2	0	1	446	**Baby Love** Supremes
87	9	2	0	1	447	**I Just Can't Stop Loving You** Michael Jackson
82	8	2	0	1	448	**Happy Talk** Captain Sensible
68	8	2	0	0	449	**Lady Madonna** Beatles
82	9	2	0	0	450	**A Little Peace** Nicole
57	12	2	0	0	451	**Great Balls Of Fire** Jerry Lee Lewis
59	20	1	6	1	452	**Smoke Gets In Your Eyes** Platters
68	35	1	5	1	453	**Albatross** Fleetwood Mac
73	24	1	5	0	454	**Welcome Home** Peters and Lee
76	18	1	5	0	455	**Don't Cry For Me Argentina** Julie Covington
60	15	1	4	0	456	**Do You Mind** Anthony Newley
70	20	1	4	0	457	**Tears Of A Clown** Smokey Robinson and the Miracles
77	12	1	3	1	458	**Angelo** Brotherhood Of Man
61	15	1	3	1	459	**Sailor** Petula Clark
65	22	1	3	1	460	**It's Not Unusual** Tom Jones
86	11	1	3	1	461	**Caravan Of Love** Housemartins
64	15	1	3	0	462	**It's All Over Now** Rolling Stones
75	11	1	3	0	463	**Barbados** Typically Tropical
78	19	1	3	0	464	**Hit Me With Your Rhythm Stick** Ian and the Blockheads
73	14	1	3	0	465	**The Twelfth Of Never** Donny Osmond
69	19	1	3	0	466	**I'll Never Fall In Love Again** Bobbie Gentry
72	12	1	3	0	467	**You Wear It Well** Rod Stewart
87	15	1	3	0	468	**Respectable** Mel and Kim
65	14	1	3	0	469	**Keep On Running** Spencer Davis Group
76	9	1	3	0	470	**Forever And Ever** Slik
80	11	1	3	0	471	**Together We Are Beautiful** Fern Kinney
73	16	1	2	4	472	**You Won't Find Another Fool Like Me** New Seekers
56	20	1	2	3	473	**Rock And Roll Waltz** Kay Starr
59	14	1	2	2	474	**Here Comes Summer** Jerry Keller
62	26	1	2	2	475	**Nut Rocker** B. Bumble and the Stingers
70	22	1	2	2	476	**Yellow River** Christie
57	14	1	2	2	477	**Rock-A-Billy** Guy Mitchell
77	16	1	2	2	478	**Yes Sir I Can Boogie** Baccara

Siedah Garrett (left) received a credit on the sleeve of Michael Jackson's I Just Can't Stop Loving You, but not on the label

Year	Weeks on Chart	Weeks at			Rank	Title Artist
		No 1	No 2	No 3		
61	18	1	2	2	479	**Reach For The Stars/Climb Ev'ry Mountain** Shirley Bassey
75	11	1	2	2	480	**Tears On My Pillow** Johnny Nash
85	13	1	2	2	481	**I Got You Babe** UB40 featuring guest vocals by Chrissie Hynde
79	18	1	2	2	482	**Cars** Gary Numan
61	21	1	2	1	483	**Well I Ask You** Eden Kane
77	14	1	2	1	484	**Lucille** Kenny Rogers
69	34	1	2	1	485	**Je T'Aime ... Moi Non Plus** Jane Birkin and Serge Gainsbourg
85	21	1	2	1	486	**Move Closer** Phyllis Nelson
86	15	1	2	1	487	**Rock Me Amadeus** Falco
68	15	1	2	1	488	**I've Gotta Get A Message To You** Bee Gees
78	11	1	2	1	489	**Figaro** Brotherhood Of Man
61	16	1	2	1	490	**You're Driving Me Crazy** Temperance Seven
74	13	1	2	1	491	**Annie's Song** John Denver
64	15	1	2	1	492	**Juliet** Four Pennies
73	15	1	2	1	493	**Rubber Bullets** 10 C.C.
73	14	1	2	1	494	**Can The Can** Suzi Quatro
83	15	1	2	1	495	**Billie Jean** Michael Jackson
68	12	1	2	1	496	**Legend Of Xanadu** Dave Dee, Dozy, Beaky, Mick and Tich
76	11	1	2	1	497	**No Charge** J.J. Barrie
86	15	1	2	1	498	**True Blue** Madonna
80	10	1	2	1	499	**Start** Jam
74	11	1	2	1	500	**Jealous Mind** Alvin Stardust
77	10	1	2	1	501	**Show You The Way To Go** Jacksons
68	14	1	2	1	502	**Fire** Crazy World Of Arthur Brown
85	13	1	2	1	503	**There Must Be An Angel (Playing With My Heart)** Eurythmics
84	13	1	2	1	504	**I Should Have Known Better** Jim Diamond
77	11	1	2	1	505	**Uptown Top Ranking** Althia and Donna
66	12	1	2	1	506	**All Or Nothing** Small Faces
87	10	1	2	1	507	**Who's That Girl** Madonna
66	17	1	2	1	508	**Out Of Time** Chris Farlowe
78	13	1	2	0	509	**Dreadlock Holiday** 10 C.C.
67	13	1	2	0	510	**Ballad Of Bonnie And Clyde** Georgie Fame
65	15	1	2	0	511	**Concrete And Clay** Unit Four Plus Two
85	11	1	2	0	512	**If I Was** Midge Ure
80	15	1	2	0	513	**(Just Like) Starting Over** John Lennon
70	13	1	2	0	514	**Voodoo Chile** Jimi Hendrix Experience

Eurythmics

Year	Weeks on Chart	Weeks at No 1	No 2	No 3	Rank	Title	Artist
65	10	1	2	0	515	**Tired Of Waiting For You**	Kinks
66	10	1	2	0	516	**Paint It Black**	Rolling Stones
79	11	1	2	0	517	**Video Killed The Radio Star**	Buggles
65	11	1	2	0	518	**Where Are You Now (My Love)** Jackie Trent	
68	13	1	2	0	519	**With A Little Help From My Friends** Joe Cocker	
82	8	1	2	0	520	**My Camera Never Lies**	Bucks Fizz
68	36	1	1	3	521	**I Pretend**	Des O'Connor
65	14	1	1	3	522	**Make It Easy On Yourself** Walker Brothers	
72	13	1	1	3	523	**Take Me Bak 'Ome**	Slade
60	19	1	1	2	524	**Shakin' All Over** Johnny Kidd and the Pirates	
64	19	1	1	2	525	**Diane**	Bachelors
69	19	1	1	2	526	**Dizzy**	Tommy Roe
62	15	1	1	2	527	**Dance On**	Shadows
64	14	1	1	2	528	**Go Now**	Moody Blues
69	24	1	1	2	529	**Israelites**	Desmond Dekker and the Aces
79	10	1	1	2	530	**Walking On The Moon**	Police
63	12	1	1	2	531	**(You're The) Devil In Disguise** Elvis Presley	
81	14	1	1	2	532	**Begin The Beguine (Volver A Empezar)** Julio Iglesias	
73	10	1	1	2	533	**Angel Fingers**	Wizzard
61	14	1	1	2	534	**Michael**	Highwaymen
82	10	1	1	2	535	**Oh Julie**	Shakin' Stevens
60	17	1	1	1	536	**Poor Me**	Adam Faith
77	11	1	1	1	537	**Float On**	Floaters
68	14	1	1	1	538	**Do It Again**	Beach Boys
81	21	1	1	1	539	**The Model/Computer Love**	Kraftwerk
65	14	1	1	1	540	**The Minute You're Gone**	Cliff Richard
63	16	1	1	1	541	**Foot Tapper**	Shadows
81	12	1	1	1	542	**Japanese Boy**	Aneka
74	12	1	1	1	543	**The Streak**	Ray Stevens
78	13	1	1	1	544	**Da Ya Think I'm Sexy**	Rod Stewart
80	9	1	1	1	545	**Call Me**	Blondie
68	12	1	1	1	546	**Blackberry Way**	Move
74	9	1	1	1	547	**Always Yours**	Gary Glitter
81	13	1	1	1	548	**Every Little Thing She Does Is Magic** Police	
82	12	1	1	1	549	**I've Never Been To Me**	Charlene
75	10	1	1	1	550	**D.I.V.O.R.C.E.**	Billy Connolly
65	15	1	1	0	551	**King Of The Road**	Roger Miller
58	16	1	1	0	552	**The Day The Rains Came**	Jane Morgan

Shakin´ Stevens

Year	Weeks on Chart	Weeks at No 1	No 2	No 3	Rank	Title Artist
56	15	1	1	0	553	**Singing The Blues** Tommy Steele
74	11	1	1	0	554	**Ms Grace** Tymes
66	13	1	1	0	555	**You Don't Have To Say You Love Me** Dusty Springfield
64	28	1	1	0	556	**House Of The Rising Sun** Animals
76	12	1	0	3	557	**The Roussos Phenomenon (EP)** Demis Roussos
61	12	1	0	2	558	**Kon-Tiki** Shadows
60	12	1	0	2	559	**Starry Eyed** Michael Holliday
84	12	1	0	2	560	**The Power Of Love** Frankie Goes To Hollywood
74	10	1	0	2	561	**Sad Sweet Dreamer** Sweet Sensation
83	13	1	0	2	562	**Candy Girl** New Edition
64	12	1	0	2	563	**Little Red Rooster** Rolling Stones
74	11	1	0	1	564	**Down Down** Status Quo
61	14	1	0	1	565	**On The Rebound** Floyd Cramer
66	11	1	0	0	566	**Get Away** Georgie Fame and the Blue Flames
57	21		7	2	567	**Love Letters In The Sand** Pat Boone
61	16		6	2	568	**Are You Sure** Allisons
69	23		6	1	569	**Ruby Don't Take Your Love To Town** Kenny Rogers and the First Edition
78	17		6	1	570	**The Smurf Song** Father Abraham and the Smurfs
77	13		6	0	571	**The Floral Dance** Brighouse and Rastrick Brass Band
76	14		5	2	572	**A Little Bit More** Dr. Hook
71	15		5	2	573	**Jeepster** T. Rex
57	16		5	1	574	**Don't Forbid Me** Pat Boone
70	25		5	1	575	**All Right Now** Free
60	30		5	1	576	**As Long As He Needs Me** Shirley Bassey
84	22		5	1	577	**Last Christmas/Everything She Wants** Wham!
57	15		5	0	578	**Ma He's Making Eyes At Me** Johnny Otis Show
71	19		5	0	579	**Never Ending Song Of Love** New Seekers
60	18		4	2	580	**Save The Last Dance For Me** Drifters
71	21		4	2	581	**Pushbike Song** Mixtures
56	17		4	1	582	**Zambesi** Lou Busch
62	19		4	1	583	**Speedy Gonzales** Pat Boone
67	25		4	1	584	**I'll Never Fall In Love Again** Tom Jones
57	15		4	1	585	**Party** Elvis Presley
81	14		4	1	586	**Vienna** Ultravox
66	15		4	1	587	**Morningtown Ride** Seekers

Year	Weeks on Chart	Weeks at No 1	No 2	No 3	Rank	Title Artist
87	14		4	1	588	**Can't Be With You Tonight** Judy Boucher
58	14		4	1	589	**Tom Hark** Elias and his Zigzag Jive Flutes
67	29		4	0	590	**There Goes My Everything** Engelbert Humperdinck
62	35		4	0	591	**Let's Dance** Chris Montez
81	12		4	0	592	**You Drive Me Crazy** Shakin' Stevens
81	12		4	0	593	**Daddy's Home** Cliff Richard
87	14		4	0	594	**Got My Mind Set On You** George Harrison
79	10		4	0	595	**I Have A Dream** Abba
56	35		3	4	596	**Hound Dog** Elvis Presley
70	14		3	4	597	**When I'm Dead And Gone** McGuinness Flint
56	15		3	3	598	**Green Door** Frankie Vaughan
63	21		3	3	599	**From A Jack To A King** Ned Miller
57	18		3	3	600	**Banana Boat Song** Harry Belafonte
63	22		3	3	601	**Please Please Me** Beatles
56	17		3	3	602	**Lost John/Stewball** Lonnie Donegan
62	17		3	1	603	**I'm Looking Out The Window/Do You Wanna Dance** Cliff Richard and the Shadows
65	16		3	2	604	**Wind Me Up (Let Me Go)** Cliff Richard
72	18		3	2	605	**Crazy Horses** Osmonds
58	14		3	2	606	**Volare** Dean Martin
72	16		3	2	607	**American Pie** Don McLean
72	13		3	2	608	**Beg Steal Or Borrow** New Seekers
62	15		3	2	609	**Tell Me What He Said** Helen Shapiro
83	21		3	2	610	**I.O.U.** Freeez
72	20		3	2	611	**Mother Of Mine** Neil Reid
79	14		3	2	612	**Dance Away** Roxy Music
80	18		3	2	613	**D.I.S.C.O.** Ottawan
75	10		3	2	614	**The Trail Of The Lonesome Pine** Laurel and Hardy with the Avalon Boys
83	13		3	1	615	**Love Of The Common People** Paul Young
75	21		3	1	616	**You Sexy Thing** Hot Chocolate
68	15		3	1	617	**A Man Without Love** Engelbert Humperdinck
68	17		3	1	618	**Delilah** Tom Jones
73	14		3	1	619	**Hello Hello I'm Back Again** Gary Glitter
85	22		3	1	620	**Axel F** Harold Faltermeyer
79	12		3	1	621	**Oliver's Army** Elvis Costello and the Attractions
71	13		3	1	622	**Brown Sugar/Bitch/Let It Rock** Rolling Stones

Abba

Year	Weeks on Chart	Weeks at No 1	No 2	No 3	Rank	Title Artist
67	12		3	1	623	**Magical Mystery Tour (Double EP)** Beatles
84	31		3	1	624	**Ghostbusters** Ray Parker Jr.
85	14		3	1	625	**Love And Pride** King
77	14		3	1	626	**Black Is Black** La Belle Epoque
73	11		3	1	627	**Part Of The Union** Strawbs
84	14		3	1	628	**Against All Odds (Take A Look At Me Now)** Phil Collins
70	13		3	1	629	**Patches** Clarence Carter
62	28		3	1	630	**Loco-Motion** Little Eva
78	14		3	1	631	**Denis** Blondie
77	12		3	1	632	**Magic Fly** Space
85	19		3	1	633	**Take On Me** a-ha
72	15		3	1	634	**Rock 'n' Roll (Parts 1 and 2)** Gary Glitter
69	14		3	1	635	**Goodbye** Mary Hopkin
56	9		3	1	636	**The Ballad Of Davy Crockett** Bill Hayes
79	11		3	1	637	**Some Girls** Racey
83	11		3	1	638	**My Oh My** Slade
71	14		3	1	639	**Bridget The Midget (The Queen Of The Blues)** Ray Stevens
73	9		3	1	640	**Ballroom Blitz** Sweet
66	10		3	1	641	**I Can't Let Go** Hollies
71	12		3	1	642	**Witch Queen Of New Orleans** Redbone
61	15		3	0	643	**Downtown** Petula Clark
69	11		3	0	644	**In The Ghetto** Elvis Presley
60	15		3	0	645	**Voice In The Wilderness** Cliff Richard and the Shadows
69	13		3	0	646	**Give Peace A Chance** John Lennon/Plastic Ono Band
83	16		3	0	647	**All Night Long (All Night)** Lionel Richie
63	13		3	0	648	**It's All In The Game** Cliff Richard
60	16		3	0	649	**Cradle Of Love** Johnny Preston
80	11		3	0	650	**No Doubt About It** Hot Chocolate
58	14		3	0	651	**Come Prima** Marino Marini
73	11		3	0	652	**Hell Raiser** Sweet
73	14		3	0	653	**Let Me In** Osmonds
64	11		3	0	654	**Bits And Pieces** Dave Clark Five
74	13		3	0	655	**Kissin' In The Back Row Of The Movies** Drifters
86	13		3	0	656	**On My Own** Patti Labelle and Michael McDonald
65	13		3	0	657	**Heart Full Of Soul** Yardbirds
74	8		3	0	658	**Teenage Rampage** Sweet
67	14		3	0	659	**Penny Lane/Strawberry Fields Forever** Beatles
77	8		3	0	660	**Going In With My Eyes Open** David Soul

Year	Weeks on Chart	No 1	No 2	No 3	Rank	Title Artist
61	55		3	0	661	**Stranger On The Shore** Mr. Acker Bilk with the Leon Young String Chorale
76	10		3	0	662	**Let'Em In** Wings
65	17		3	0	663	**Almost There** Andy Williams
84	10		3	0	664	**Hole In My Shoe** neil
72	10		3	0	665	**Children Of The Revolution** T. Rex
81	17		3	0	666	**Happy Birthday** Altered Images
77	11		3	0	667	**We Are The Champions** Queen
68	15		3	0	668	**Son Of Hickory Holler's Tramp** O.C. Smith
85	16		3	0	669	**A View To A Kill** Duran Duran
85	13		3	0	670	**Holding Out For A Hero** Bonnie Tyler
82	10		3	0	671	**Mirror Man** Human League
66	8		3	0	672	**Nineteenth Nervous Breakdown** Rolling Stones
55	13		2	5	673	**Love Is A Many Splendoured Thing** Four Aces
59	16		2	4	674	**Battle Of New Orleans** Lonnie Donegan
60	18		2	4	675	**A Mess Of Blues** Elvis Presley
68	27		2	4	676	**Honey** Bobby Goldsboro
62	19		2	3	677	**A Picture Of You** Joe Brown and the Bruvvers
56	34		2	3	678	**Heartbreak Hotel** Elvis Presley
61	44		2	3	679	**Let's Twist Again** Chubby Checker
57	17		2	3	680	**Last Train To San Fernando** Johnny Duncan and the Bluegrass Boys
68	15		2	3	681	**Build Me Up Buttercup** Foundations
57	13		2	3	682	**Wake Up Little Susie** Everly Brothers
79	14		2	3	683	**Pop Muzik** M
69	16		2	3	684	**Saved By The Bell** Robin Gibb
80	13		2	3	685	**Funky Town** Lipps Inc
59	17		2	2	686	**A Teenager In Love** Marty Wilde
84	30		2	2	687	**Agadoo** Black Lace
62	14		2	2	688	**Dream Baby** Roy Orbison
85	15		2	2	689	**Everybody Wants To Rule The World** Tears For Fears
64	14		2	2	690	**I'm Gonna Be Strong** Gene Pitney
87	15		2	2	691	**Under The Boardwalk** Bruce Willis
63	15		2	2	692	**Do You Want To Know A Secret** Billy J. Kramer and the Dakotas
78	15		2	2	693	**Substitute** Clout
68	12		2	2	694	**Eloise** Barry Ryan
66	14		2	2	695	**God Only Knows** Beach Boys
71	15		2	2	696	**CoCo** Sweet
70	27		2	2	697	**Black Night** Deep Purple

Gary Glitter

Year	Weeks on Chart	Weeks at No 1	No 2	No 3	Rank	Title Artist
17	11		2	2	698	**Do You Wanna Touch Me (Oh Yeah)** Gary Glitter
86	28		2	2	699	**So Macho/Cruising** Sinitta
81	11		2	2	700	**Hooked On Classics** Royal Philharmonic Orchestra Cond. Louis Clark
67	11		2	2	701	**Waterloo Sunset** Kinks
70	14		2	2	702	**Neanderthal Man** Hotlegs
76	23		2	2	703	**Can't Get By Without You** Real Thing
86	14		2	2	704	**We Don't Have To ...** Jermaine Stewart
79	14		2	2	705	**Silly Games** Janet Kay
83	10		2	2	706	**Say Say Say** Paul McCartney and Michael Jackson
72	13		2	2	707	**Donna** 10 C.C.
67	14		2	2	708	**Everybody Knows** Dave Clark Five
61	16		2	1	709	**Hello Mary Lou/Travellin' Man** Ricky Nelson
71	12		2	1	710	**Another Day** Paul McCartney
69	16		2	1	711	**Oh Well** Fleetwood Mac
63	17		2	1	712	**Atlantis** Shadows
64	17		2	1	713	**Someone Someone** Brian Poole and the Tremeloes
58	14		2	1	714	**Big Man** Four Preps
67	13		2	1	715	**Flowers In The Rain** Move
80	14		2	1	716	**Dance Yourself Dizzy** Liquid Gold
63	14		2	1	717	**Then He Kissed Me** Crystals
81	12		2	1	718	**Chi Mai (Theme from the TV Series _The Life & Times of David Lloyd George_)** Ennio Morricone
69	14		2	1	719	**(Call Me) Number One** Tremeloes
82	12		2	1	720	**Golden Brown** Stranglers
75	11		2	1	721	**There's A Whole Lot Of Lovin'** Guys and Dolls
81	13		2	1	722	**Kids In America** Kim Wilde
78	10		2	1	723	**Rasputin** Boney M
86	11		2	1	724	**Rain Or Shine** Five Star
75	10		2	1	725	**Loving You** Minnie Ripperton
70	15		2	1	726	**You Can Get It If You Really Want** Desmond Dekker
82	11		2	1	727	**Abracadabra** Steve Miller Band
74	10		2	1	728	**This Town Ain't Big Enough For Both Of Us** Sparks
84	11		2	1	729	**Joanna/Tonight** Kool And The Gang
78	11		2	1	730	**Hopelessly Devoted To You** Olivia Newton-John
72	10		2	1	731	**Back Off Boogaloo** Ringo Starr

Year	Weeks on Chart	Weeks at No 1	Weeks at No 2	Weeks at No 3	Rank	Title Artist
65	13		2	1	732	**My Generation** Who
83	14		2	1	733	**Bad Boys** Wham!
74	12		2	1	734	**Killer Queen** Queen
76	10		2	1	735	**When Forever Has Gone** Demis Roussos
74	12		2	1	736	**You Ain't Seen Nothing Yet** Bachman-Turner Overdrive
63	11		2	1	737	**I'm Telling You Now** Freddie and the Dreamers
74	6		2	1	738	**Far Far Away** Slade
81	28		2	1	739	**Birdie Song (Birdie Dance)** Tweets
80	12		2	1	740	**Upside Down** Diana Ross
79	14		2	1	741	**Crazy Little Thing Called Love** Queen
79	9		2	1	742	**Chiquitita** Abba
82	13		2	1	743	**Heartbreaker** Dionne Warwick
88	9		2	1	744	**Beat Dis** Bomb The Bass
69	12		2	1	745	**Oh Happy Day** Edwin Hawkins Singers
67	10		2	1	746	**Matthew And Son** Cat Stevens
83	11		2	1	747	**They Don't Know** Tracey Ullman
75	10		2	1	748	**Fox On The Run** Sweet
82	12		2	1	749	**Mickey** Toni Basil
66	12		2	1	750	**Bend It** Dave Dee, Dozy, Beaky, Mick and Tich
71	17		2	1	751	**I Did What I Did For Maria** Tony Christie
77	10		2	1	752	**Red Light Spells Danger** Billy Ocean
86	14		2	1	753	**You Keep Me Hangin' On** Kim Wilde
84	10		2	1	754	**A Love Worth Waiting For** Shakin' Stevens
66	13		2	1	755	**Daydream** Lovin' Spoonful
83	9		2	1	756	**Gold** Spandau Ballet
87	10		2	1	757	**Full Metal Jacket (I Wanna Be Your Drill Instructor)** Abigail Mead and Nigel Goulding
84	12		2	1	758	**Let's Hear It For The Boy** Deniece Williams
87	9		2	1	759	**What Have I Done To Deserve This** Pet Shop Boys and Dusty Springfield
74	9		2	1	760	**The Cat Crept In** Mud
67	15		2	0	761	**Excerpt from 'A Teenage Opera'** Keith West
58	16		2	0	762	**To Know Him Is To Love Him** Teddy Bears
73	17		2	0	763	**Yesterday Once More** Carpenters
84	15		2	0	764	**Automatic** Pointer Sisters
74	12		2	0	765	**Streets Of London** Ralph McTell
80	18		2	0	766	**Antmusic** Adam and the Ants
64	15		2	0	767	**I'm The One** Gerry and the Pacemakers

Pet Shop Boys and Dusty Springfield

Year	Weeks on Chart	Weeks at No 1	No 2	No 3	Rank	Title Artist
58	11		2	0	768	**Hard Headed Woman** Elvis Presley
76	10		2	0	769	**You See The Trouble With Me** Barry White
84	9		2	0	770	**Radio Ga Ga** Queen
73	15		2	0	771	**(Dancing On) A Saturday Night** Barry Blue
83	12		2	0	772	**Words** F.R. David
66	28		2	0	773	**When A Man Loves A Woman** Percy Sledge
72	12		2	0	774	**Seaside Shuffle** Terry Dactyl and the Dinosaurs
64	13		2	0	775	**Rag Doll** Four Seasons
80	11		2	0	776	**What You're Proposin'** Status Quo
69	12		2	0	777	**My Sentimental Friend** Herman's Hermits
75	12		2	0	778	**Glass Of Champagne** Sailor
78	10		2	0	779	**Love Don't Live Here Anymore** Rose Royce
80	11		2	0	780	**One Day I'll Fly Away** Randy Crawford
81	10		2	0	781	**Stars On 45 (Volume 2)** Starsound
87	12		2	0	782	**Heartache** Pepsi and Shirlie
85	17		2	0	783	**Holding Back The Years** Simply Red
85	10		2	0	784	**That Ole Devil Called Love** Alison Moyet
66	12		2	0	785	**Stop Stop Stop** Hollies
87	10		2	0	786	**When I Fall In Love/My Arms Keep Missing You** Rick Astley
82	7		2	0	787	**The Shakin' Stevens EP** Shakin' Stevens
79	9		2	0	788	**In The Navy** Village People
87	9		2	0	789	**Fairytale Of New York** Pogues featuring Kirsty MacColl
88	9		2	0	790	**Together Forever** Rick Astley
85	11		2	0	791	**Welcome To The Pleasuredome** Frankie Goes To Hollywood
61	10		2	0	792	**Wild Wind** John Leyton
64	14		2	0	793	**All Day And All Of The Night** Kinks
83	9		2	0	794	**Church Of The Poison Mind** Culture Club
87	12		2	0	795	**Faith** George Michael
82	7		2	0	796	**The Bitterest Pill (I Ever Had To Swallow)** Jam
57	16		2	0	797	**Be My Girl** Jim Dale
79	11		2	0	798	**With You I'm Born Again** Billy Preston and Syreeta
57	27		1	4	799	**When I Fall In Love** Nat 'King' Cole
58	22		1	4	800	**Return To Me** Dean Martin

Year	Weeks on Chart	No 1	No 2	No 3	Rank	Title Artist
64	17		1	4	801	**I Believe** Bachelors
63	17		1	4	802	**Hippy Hippy Shake** Swinging Blue Jeans
75	14		1	4	803	**The Last Farewell** Roger Whittaker
68	18		1	4	804	**Jesamine** Casuals
81	14		1	4	805	**Stars On 45** Starsound
56	15		1	3	806	**Walk Hand In Hand** Tony Martin
57	17		1	3	807	**Tammy** Debbie Reynolds
77	13		1	3	808	**Fanfare For The Common Man** Emerson Lake and Palmer
62	17		1	3	809	**Swiss Maid** Del Shannon
61	13		1	3	810	**Big Bad John** Jimmy Dean
70	18		1	3	811	**Groovin' With Mr. Bloe** Mr. Bloe
72	11		1	3	812	**Solid Gold Easy Action** T. Rex
66	17		1	3	813	**What Would I Be** Val Doonican
69	14		1	3	814	**Man Of The World** Fleetwood Mac
74	13		1	3	815	**The Air That I Breathe** Hollies
78	13		1	3	816	**Boy From New York City** Darts
58	16		1	3	817	**Bird Dog** Everly Brothers
64	18		1	3	818	**My Boy Lollipop** Millie
71	19		1	3	819	**Did You Ever** Nancy and Lee
85	15		1	3	820	**Crazy For You** Madonna
60	13		1	3	821	**Someone Else's Baby** Adam Faith
75	11		1	3	822	**Three Steps To Heaven** Showaddywaddy
67	17		1	3	823	**Dedicated To The One I Love** Mamas and the Papas
76	12		1	3	824	**You Make Me Feel Like Dancing** Leo Sayer
71	15		1	3	825	**Indiana Wants Me** R. Dean Taylor
79	12		1	3	826	**Bang Bang** B.A. Robertson
70	15		1	3	827	**Let's Work Together** Canned Heat
65	14		1	3	828	**You've Got Your Troubles** Fortunes
69	17		1	3	829	**I'm Gonna Make You Mine** Lou Christie
82	9		1	3	830	**Torch** Soft Cell
75	12		1	3	831	**I Believe In Father Christmas** Greg Lake
70	14		1	2	832	**Lola** Kinks
71	17		1	2	833	**Tweedle Dee Tweedle Dum** Middle Of The Road
60	18		1	2	834	**Because They're Young** Duane Eddy
60	19		1	2	835	**Mama/Robot Man** Connie Francis
78	12		1	2	836	**Come Back My Love** Darts
78	15		1	2	837	**Sandy** John Travolta
78	11		1	2	838	**It's Raining** Darts
62	17		1	2	839	**Things** Bobby Darin
77	13		1	2	840	**Ma Baker** Boney M
74	14		1	2	841	**Hey Rock And Roll** Showaddywaddy

Adam Faith

Year	Weeks on Chart	Weeks at No 1	No 2	No 3	Rank	Title Artist
63	13		1	2	842	**Scarlett O'Hara** Jet Harris and Tony Meehan
57	20		1	2	843	**We Will Make Love** Russ Hamilton
67	12		1	2	844	**Alternate Title** Monkees
67	14		1	2	845	**Hole In My Shoe** Traffic
72	13		1	2	846	**Sylvia's Mother** Dr. Hook and the Medicine Show
66	13		1	2	847	**I'm A Boy** Who
76	10		1	2	848	**Love Really Hurts Without You** Billy Ocean
77	11		1	2	849	**Ain't Gonna Bump No More (With No Big Fat Woman)** Joe Tex
72	13		1	2	850	**The Jean Genie** David Bowie
66	14		1	2	851	**A Groovy Kind Of Love** Mindbenders
77	14		1	2	852	**Boogie Nights** Heatwave
74	14		1	2	853	**You Make Me Feel Brand New** Stylistics
65	14		1	2	854	**The Price Of Love** Everly Brothers
70	12		1	2	855	**Question** Moody Blues
87	11		1	2	856	**Hold Me Now** Johnny Logan
73	13		1	2	857	**The Show Must Go On** Leo Sayer
72	17		1	2	858	**Could It Be Forever/Cherish** David Cassidy
76	10		1	2	859	**Convoy** C.W. McCall
82	11		1	2	860	**Zoom** Fat Larry's Band
73	8		1	2	861	**My Frend Stan** Slade
77	10		1	2	862	**You Got What It Takes** Showaddywaddy
66	12		1	2	863	**Wild Thing** Troggs
83	9		1	2	864	**Electric Avenue** Eddy Grant
83	14		1	2	865	**Sweet Dreams (Are Made Of This)** Eurythmics
69	15		1	2	866	**Don't Forget To Remember** Bee Gees
73	15		1	2	867	**Paper Roses** Marie Osmond
65	12		1	2	868	**Here Comes The Night** Them
68	16		1	2	869	**Simon Says** 1910 Fruitgum Co.
59	15		1	2	870	**Baby Face** Little Richard
67	16		1	2	871	**I'm Coming Home** Tom Jones
76	11		1	2	872	**Silly Love Songs** Wings
86	14		1	2	873	**I Can't Wait** Nu Shooz
65	12		1	2	874	**If You Gotta Go Go Now** Manfred Mann
78	11		1	2	875	**I Wonder Why** Showaddywaddy
82	9		1	2	876	**Save A Prayer** Duran Duran
71	12		1	2	877	**Don't Let It Die** Hurricane Smith
84	14		1	2	878	**Wild Boys** Duran Duran
74	10		1	2	879	**Born With A Smile On My Face** Stephanie De Sykes and Rain
62	12		1	2	880	**It'll Be Me** Cliff Richard and the Shadows

Year	Weeks on Chart	Weeks at No 1	Weeks at No 2	Weeks at No 3	Rank	Title Artist
75	12		1	2	881	**Please Mr. Postman** Carpenters
79	11		1	2	882	**Cool For Cats** Squeeze
84	8		1	2	883	**The War Song** Culture Club
68	18		1	2	884	**Ain't Got No—I Got Life/ Do What You Gotta Do** Nina Simone
80	9		1	2	885	**Coming Up** Paul McCartney
87	12		1	2	886	**Wipeout** Fat Boys and the Beach Boys
81	10		1	2	887	**More Than In Love** Kate Robbins and Beyond
72	25		1	1	888	**Happy Xmas (War Is Over)** John and Yoko/Plastic Ono Band with the Harlem Community Choir
76	9		1	1	889	**Somebody To Love** Queen
58	17		1	1	890	**A Wonderful Time Up There** Pat Boone
59	15		1	1	891	**('Til) I Kissed You** Everly Brothers
83	14		1	1	892	**Flashdance . . . What A Feeling** Irene Cara
68	16		1	1	893	**Lazy Sunday** Small Faces
62	12		1	1	894	**Hey! Baby** Bruce Channel
72	16		1	1	895	**Come What May** Vicky Leandros
75	10		1	1	896	**Misty** Ray Stevens
81	10		1	1	897	**In The Air Tonight** Phil Collins
65	15		1	1	898	**True Love Ways** Peter and Gordon
69	13		1	1	899	**Yester-Me Yester-You Yesterday** Stevie Wonder
76	13		1	1	900	**Young Hearts Run Free** Candi Staton
66	13		1	1	901	**Black Is Black** Los Bravos
56	9		1	1	902	**The Tender Trap** Frank Sinatra
84	15		1	1	903	**No More Lonely Nights** Paul McCartney
80	10		1	1	904	**Masterblaster (Jammin')** Stevie Wonder
85	14		1	1	905	**Kayleigh** Marillion
87	12		1	1	906	**A Boy From Nowhere** Tom Jones
83	18		1	1	907	**I Won't Let The Sun Go Down On Me** Nik Kershaw
66	14		1	1	908	**You Were On My Mind** Crispian St. Peters
84	9		1	1	909	**You Take Me Up** Thompson Twins
73	21		1	1	910	**My Coo-Ca-Choo** Alvin Stardust
55	11		1	1	911	**Meet Me On The Corner** Max Bygraves
74	12		1	1	912	**I'm Leaving It (All) Up To You** Donny and Marie Osmond
72	13		1	1	913	**Gudbuy T'Jane** Slade
67	20		1	1	914	**It Must Be Him (Seul Sur Son Etoile)** Vikki Carr
67	17		1	1	915	**Edelweiss** Vince Hill
86	14		1	1	916	**In The Army Now** Status Quo
62	15		1	1	917	**Hey Little Girl** Del Shannon

Year	Weeks on Chart	Weeks at No 1	No 2	No 3	Rank	Title Artist
66	12		1	1	918	**Gimme Some Lovin'** Spencer Davis Group
75	10		1	1	919	**Love Is The Drug** Roxy Music
86	11		1	1	920	**Walk Of Life** Dire Straits
66	11		1	1	921	**Sunshine Superman** Donovan
75	8		1	1	922	**Moonlighting** Leo Sayer
70	16		1	1	923	**Leavin' On A Jet Plane** Peter, Paul and Mary
65	12		1	1	924	**We Gotta Get Out Of This Place** Animals
66	14		1	1	925	**I Can't Control Myself** Troggs
56	9		1	1	926	**All Star Hit Parade** Winifred Atwell/Dave King/Joan Regan/Lita Roza/Dickie Valentine/David Whitfield
63	13		1	1	927	**Sugar And Spice** Searchers
79	11		1	1	928	**Up The Junction** Squeeze
84	13		1	1	929	**Borderline** Madonna
83	9		1	1	930	**(Keep Feeling) Fascination** Human League
83	13		1	1	931	**Tonight I Celebrate My Love** Peabo Bryson and Roberta Flack
67	10		1	1	932	**Night Of Fear** Move
82	14		1	1	933	**Only You** Yazoo
81	11		1	1	934	**Happy Birthday** Stevie Wonder
79	8		1	1	935	**Dreaming** Blondie
70	10		1	1	936	**Let It Be** Beatles
82	11		1	1	937	**Just An Illusion** Imagination
83	8		1	1	938	**Modern Love** David Bowie
74	14		1	1	939	**The Most Beautiful Girl** Charlie Rich
77	9		1	1	940	**Sir Duke** Stevie Wonder
83	13		1	1	941	**Temptation** Heaven 17
86	12		1	1	942	**Manic Monday** Bangles
84	12		1	1	943	**Girls Just Wanna Have Fun** Cyndi Lauper
80	11		1	1	944	**More Than I Can Say** Leo Sayer
88	10		1	1	945	**Sign Your Name** Terence Trent D'Arby
82	8		1	1	946	**Private Investigations** Dire Straits
74	10		1	1	947	**Oh Yes! You're Beautiful** Gary Glitter
86	9		1	1	948	**Every Beat Of My Heart** Rod Stewart
83	15		1	1	949	**What Is Love** Howard Jones
60	15		1	1	950	**Fall In Love With You** Cliff Richard and the Shadows
64	13		1	1	951	**Just One Look** Hollies
86	17		1	1	952	**Sometimes** Erasure
61	21		1	1	953	**Midnight In Moscow** Kenny Ball and his Jazzmen

Terence Trent D'Arby

Year	Weeks on Chart	Weeks at No 1	No 2	No 3	Rank	Title Artist
66	12		1	1	954	**Semi-Detached Suburban Mr. James** Manfred Mann
65	11		1	1	955	**Game Of Love** Wayne Fontana and the Mindbenders
84	21		1	1	956	**Holiday** Madonna
66	15		1	1	957	**Sloop John B.** Beach Boys
63	14		1	1	958	**Don't Talk To Him** Cliff Richard and the Shadows
87	12		1	1	959	**Call Me** Spagna
85	10		1	1	960	**1999/Little Red Corvette** Prince and the Revolution
...	...	...	...	...		
80	12		1	1	961	**And The Beat Goes On** Whispers
60	11		1	1	962	**Wonderful World** Sam Cooke
67	15		1	1	963	**This Is My Song** Harry Secombe
86	10		1	1	964	**Starting Together** Su Pollard
61	13		1	1	965	**Lazy River** Bobby Darin
87	15		1	1	966	**When Will I Be Famous** Bros
60	30		1	1	967	**Theme From 'A Summer Place'** Percy Faith
82	10		1	1	968	**A Winter's Tale** David Essex
83	8		1	1	969	**China Girl** David Bowie
86	9		1	1	970	**Absolute Beginners** David Bowie
...	...	...	...	...		
81	8		1	1	971	**Invisible Sun** Police
81	6		1	1	972	**O Superman** Laurie Anderson
68	21		1	0	973	**Little Arrows** Leapy Lee
70	13		1	0	974	**I Want You Back** Jackson Five
70	20		1	0	975	**Ride A White Swan** T. Rex
76	11		1	0	976	**You Just Might See Me Cry** Our Kid
69	24		1	0	977	**Gentle On My Mind** Dean Martin
56	15		1	0	978	**A Tear Fell** Teresa Brewer
87	8		1	0	979	**Crockett's Theme** Jan Hammer
61	12		1	0	980	**Jealousy** Billy Fury
...	...	...	...	...		
74	13		1	0	981	**Never Can Say Goodbye** Gloria Gaynor
58	17		1	0	982	**Move It** Cliff Richard and the Drifters
58	9		1	0	983	**Lollipop** Mudlarks
70	14		1	0	984	**Knock Knock Who's There** Mary Hopkin
69	14		1	0	985	**Suspicious Minds** Elvis Presley
58	15		1	0	986	**King Creole** Elvis Presley
69	13		1	0	987	**Boom Bang-A-Bang** Lulu
58	11		1	0	988	**Don't** Elvis Presley
73	9		1	0	989	**Cindy Incidentally** Faces
66	13		1	0	990	**Nobody Needs Your Love** Gene Pitney
...	...	...	...	...		
71	15		1	0	991	**Till** Tom Jones
80	18		1	0	992	**Kings Of The Wild Frontier** Adam and the Ants

Lulu

Year	Weeks on Chart	Weeks at			Rank	Title Artist
		No 1	No 2	No 3		
82	11		1	0	993	**Ain't No Pleasing You** Chas and Dave
74	10		1	0	994	**Shang-A-Lang** Bay City Rollers
86	12		1	0	995	**Live To Tell** Madonna
83	10		1	0	996	**Wings Of A Dove** Madness
75	9		1	0	997	**Goodbye My Love** Glitter Band
86	11		1	0	998	**Only Love** Nana Mouskouri
78	16		1	0	999	**Can't Stand Losing You** Police
82	13		1	0	1000	**This Time (We'll Get It Right)/England We'll Fly The Flag** England World Cup Squad

England World Cup Squad

THE YEARS

A ranking of the Top 40 hits,
year by year.

1955 TOP 5

No	Title	Artist
1	Rock Around the Clock	Bill Haley and his Comets
2	Christmas Alphabet	Dickie Valentine
3	Love Is A Many Splendoured Thing	Four Aces
4	Let's Have A Ding Dong	Winifred Atwell
5	Meet Me On The Corner	Max Bygraves

1956 TOP 40

No	Title	Artist
1	Just Walkin' In The Rain	Johnnie Ray
2	Whatever Will Be Will Be	Doris Day
3	No Other Love	Ronnie Hilton
4	I'll Be Home	Pat Boone
5	Woman In Love	Frankie Laine
6	Lay Down Your Arms	Anne Shelton
7	Sixteen Tons	Tennessee Ernie Ford
8	Memories Are Made Of This	Dean Martin
9	Poor People Of Paris	Winifred Atwell
10	Why Do Fools Fall In Love	Teenagers featuring Frankie Lymon
11	It's Almost Tomorrow	Dreamweavers
12	Rock Around The Clock	Bill Haley and his Comets
13	Rock And Roll Waltz	Kay Starr
14	Zambesi	Lou Busch
15	Hound Dog	Elvis Presley
16	Lost John/Stewball	Lonnie Donegan
17	Green Door	Frankie Vaughan
18	Ballad Of Davy Crockett	Bill Hayes
19	Heartbreak Hotel	Elvis Presley
20	Walk Hand In Hand	Tony Martin
21	The Tender Trap	Frank Sinatra
22	All Star Hit Parade	Winifred Atwell/Dave King/Joan Regan/Lita Roza/Dickie Valentine/David Whitfield
23	A Tear Fell	Teresa Brewer
24	Singing The Blues	Guy Mitchell
25	Meet Me On The Corner	Max Bygraves
26	Sweet Old Fashioned Girl	Teresa Brewer
27	St. Therese Of The Roses	Malcolm Vaughan
28	Love Is A Many Splendoured Thing	Four Aces
29	Only You	Hilltoppers
30	Rockin' Through The Rye	Bill Haley and his Comets
31	Love And Marriage	Frank Sinatra
32	Bloodnok's Rock 'n' Roll/Ying Tong Song	Goons
33	My September Love	David Whitfield
34	Ballad Of Davy Crockett	Tennessee Ernie Ford
35	My Prayer	Platters
36	Rock-A-Beatin' Boogie	Bill Haley and his Comets
37	Rip It Up	Bill Haley and his Comets
38	Giddy-Up-A-Ding-Dong	Freddie Bell and the Bellboys
39	More	Jimmy Young
40	Mountain Greenery	Mel Torme

Johnnie Ray

1957 TOP 40

No	Title	Artist
1	Diana	Paul Anka
2	Young Love	Tab Hunter
3	All Shook Up	Elvis Presley
4	Mary's Boy Child	Harry Belafonte
5	Cumberland Gap	Lonnie Donegan
6	Garden Of Eden	Frankie Vaughan
7	Singing The Blues	Guy Mitchell
8	Yes Tonight Josephine	Johnnie Ray
9	That'll Be The Day	Crickets
10	Gamblin' Man/Puttin' On The Style	Lonnie Donegan
11	Butterfly	Andy Williams
12	Rock-A-Billy	Guy Mitchell
13	Singing The Blues	Tommy Steele
14	Love Letters In The Sand	Pat Boone
15	Don't Forbid Me	Pat Boone
16	Party	Elvis Presley
17	Banana Boat Song	Harry Belafonte
18	Last Train To San Fernando	Johnny Duncan and the Bluegrass Boys
19	Ma He's Making Eyes At Me	Johnny Otis Show
20	Be My Girl	Jim Dale
21	When I Fall In Love	Nat 'King' Cole
22	Tammy	Debbie Reynolds
23	We Will Make Love	Russ Hamilton
24	Wake Up Little Susie	Everly Brothers
25	Just Walkin' In The Rain	Johnnie Ray
26	Knee Deep In The Blues	Guy Mitchell
27	Friendly Persuasion	Pat Boone
28	Little Darlin'	Diamonds
29	Teddy Bear	Elvis Presley
30	Island In The Sun	Harry Belafonte
31	Long Tall Sally	Little Richard
32	I Love You Baby	Paul Anka
33	St. Therese Of The Roses	Malcolm Vaughan
34	Green Door	Frankie Vaughan
35	My Special Angel	Malcolm Vaughan
36	Around The World	Ronnie Hilton
37	Don't You Rock Me Daddy-O	Lonnie Donegan
38	True Love	Bing Crosby and Grace Kelly
39	Baby Baby	Frankie Lymon and the Teenagers
40	With All My Heart	Petula Clark

1958 TOP 40

No	Title	Artist
1	Magic Moments	Perry Como
2	All I Have To Do Is Dream/Claudette	Everly Brothers
3	Who's Sorry Now	Connie Francis
4	Carolina Moon/Stupid Cupid	Connie Francis
5	When	Kalin Twins
6	Whole Lotta Woman	Marvin Rainwater
7	Hoots Mon	Lord Rockingham's XI
8	Jailhouse Rock	Elvis Presley
9	It's All In The Game	Tommy Edwards
10	The Story Of My Life	Michael Holliday
11	On The Street Where You Live	Vic Damone
12	It's Only Make Believe	Conway Twitty
13	Great Balls Of Fire	Jerry Lee Lewis
14	Mary's Boy Child	Harry Belafonte
15	Tom Hark	Elias and his Zigzag Jive Flutes
16	Volare	Dean Martin
17	Come Prima	Marino Marini
18	Ma He's Making Eyes At Me	Johnny Otis Show
19	Big Man	Four Preps
20	Hard Headed Woman	Elvis Presley
21	Return To Me	Dean Martin
22	Bird Dog	Everly Brothers
23	A Wonderful Time Up There	Pat Boone
24	Wake Up Little Susie	Everly Brothers
25	Move It	Cliff Richard
26	Lollipop	Mudlarks
27	King Creole	Elvis Presley
28	Don't	Elvis Presley
29	Tom Dooley	Lonnie Donegan
30	You Need Hands/Tulips From Amsterdam	Max Bygraves
31	Swingin' Shepherd Blues	Ted Heath
32	Oh Boy	Crickets
33	All The Way	Frank Sinatra
34	Nairobi	Tommy Steele
35	At The Hop	Danny and the Juniors
36	Wear My Ring Around Your Neck	Elvis Presley
37	My Special Angel	Malcolm Vaughan
38	Stairway Of Love	Michael Holliday
39	Twilight Time	Platters
40	A Certain Smile	Johnny Mathis

Perry Como

1959 TOP 40

No	Title	Artist
1	Living Doll	Cliff Richard and the Shadows
2	A Fool Such As I/I Need Your Love Tonight	Elvis Presley
3	Travellin' Light	Cliff Richard and the Shadows
4	Dream Lover	Bobby Darin
5	Only Sixteen	Craig Douglas
6	As I Love You	Shirley Bassey
7	Side Saddle	Russ Conway
8	It Doesn't Matter Anymore	Buddy Holly
9	One Night/I Got Stung	Elvis Presley
10	What Do You Want	Adam Faith
11	It's Only Make Believe	Conway Twitty
12	Mack The Knife	Bobby Darin
13	What Do You Want To Make Those Eyes At Me For	Emile Ford and the Checkmates
14	Roulette	Russ Conway
15	Smoke Gets In Your Eyes	Platters
16	Here Comes Summer	Jerry Keller
17	The Day The Rains Came	Jane Morgan
18	Battle Of New Orleans	Lonnie Donegan
19	A Teenager In Love	Marty Wilde
20	Hoots Mon	Lord Rockingham's XI
21	To Know Him Is To Love Him	Teddy Bears
22	Baby Face	Little Richard
23	('Til) I Kissed You	Everly Brothers
24	Lonely Boy	Paul Anka
25	Petite Fleur	Chris Barber's Jazz Band
26	It's Late	Ricky Nelson
27	Oh Carol	Neil Sedaka
28	Kiss Me Honey Honey Kiss Me	Shirley Bassey
29	Sea Of Love	Marty Wilde
30	A Pub With No Beer	Slim Dusty
31	Red River Rock	Johnny and the Hurricanes
32	Lipstick On Your Collar	Connie Francis
33	Does Your Chewing Gum Lose Its Flavour	Lonnie Donegan
34	Tom Dooley	Lonnie Donegan
35	Donna	Marty Wilde
36	I've Waited So Long	Anthony Newley
37	Tea For Two Cha Cha	Tommy Dorsey Orchestra starring Warren Covington
38	My Happiness	Connie Francis
39	Seven Little Girls Sitting In The Back Seat	Avons
40	A Big Hunk O' Love	Elvis Presley

1960 TOP 40

No	Title	Artist
1	It's Now Or Never	Elvis Presley
2	Cathy's Clown	Everly Brothers
3	Apache	Shadows
4	Why	Anthony Newley
5	My Old Man's A Dustman	Lonnie Donegan
6	What Do You Want To Make Those Eyes At Me For	Emile Ford and the Checkmates
7	Please Don't Tease	Cliff Richard and the Shadows
8	Good Timin'	Jimmy Jones
9	Tell Laura I Love Her	Ricky Valance
10	Only The Lonely	Roy Orbison
11	Three Steps To Heaven	Eddie Cochran
12	Running Bear	Johnny Preston
13	Do You Mind	Anthony Newley
14	Shakin' All Over	Johnny Kidd and the Pirates
15	Poor Me	Adam Faith
16	I Love You	Cliff Richard and the Shadows
17	Starry Eyed	Michael Holliday
18	As Long As He Needs Me	Shirley Bassey
19	Save The Last Dance For Me	Drifters
20	Voice In The Wilderness	Cliff Richard and the Shadows
21	Cradle Of Love	Johnny Preston
22	What Do You Want	Adam Faith
23	A Mess Of Blues	Elvis Presley
24	Someone Else's Baby	Adam Faith
25	Because They're Young	Duane Eddy
26	Mama/Robot Man	Connie Francis
27	Fall In Love With You	Cliff Richard and the Shadows
28	Theme from 'A Summer Place'	Percy Faith
29	Handy Man	Jimmy Jones
30	Rocking Goose	Johnny and the Hurricanes
31	Way Down Yonder In New Orleans	Freddy Cannon
32	Delaware	Perry Como
33	Oh Carol	Neil Sedaka
34	Nine Times Out Of Ten	Cliff Richard and the Shadows
35	Strawberry Fair	Anthony Newley
36	Ain't Misbehaving	Tommy Bruce
37	Little Donkey	Nina and Frederick
38	Seven Little Girls Sitting In The Back Seat	Avons
39	On A Slow Boat To China	Emile Ford and the Checkmates
40	Stuck On You	Elvis Presley

1961 TOP 40

No	Title	Artist
1	Wooden Heart	Elvis Presley
2	Johnny Remember Me	John Leyton
3	Are You Lonesome Tonight	Elvis Presley
4	Little Sister/His Latest Flame	Elvis Presley
5	Surrender	Elvis Presley
6	Runaway	Del Shannon
7	You Don't Know	Helen Shapiro
8	Walkin' Back To Happiness	Helen Shapiro
9	Tower Of Strength	Frankie Vaughan
10	Walk Right Back/Ebony Eyes	Everly Brothers
11	Poetry In Motion	Johnny Tillotson
12	Blue Moon	Marcels
13	Temptation	Everly Brothers
14	Sailor	Petula Clark
15	Reach For The Stars/Climb Ev'ry Mountain	Shirley Bassey
16	Well I Ask You	Eden Kane
17	You're Driving Me Crazy	Temperance Seven
18	Moon River	Danny Williams
19	I Love You	Cliff Richard and the Shadows
20	Michael	Highwaymen
21	Kon-Tiki	Shadows
22	On The Rebound	Floyd Cramer
23	Are You Sure	Allisons
24	Hello Mary Lou/Travellin' Man	Ricky Nelson
25	Wild Wind	John Leyton
26	Big Bad John	Jimmy Dean
27	Save The Last Dance For Me	Drifters
28	Lazy River	Bobby Darin
29	Jealousy	Billy Fury
30	Pepe	Duane Eddy
31	Theme For A Dream	Cliff Richard and the Shadows
32	Frightened City	Shadows
33	Halfway To Paradise	Billy Fury
34	When The Girl In Your Arms Is The Girl In Your Heart	Cliff Richard
35	Take Good Care Of My Baby	Bobby Vee
36	Portrait Of My Love	Matt Monro
37	Romeo	Petula Clark
38	You're Sixteen	Johnny Burnette
39	A Girl Like You	Cliff Richard and the Shadows
40	But I Do	Clarence 'Frogman' Henry

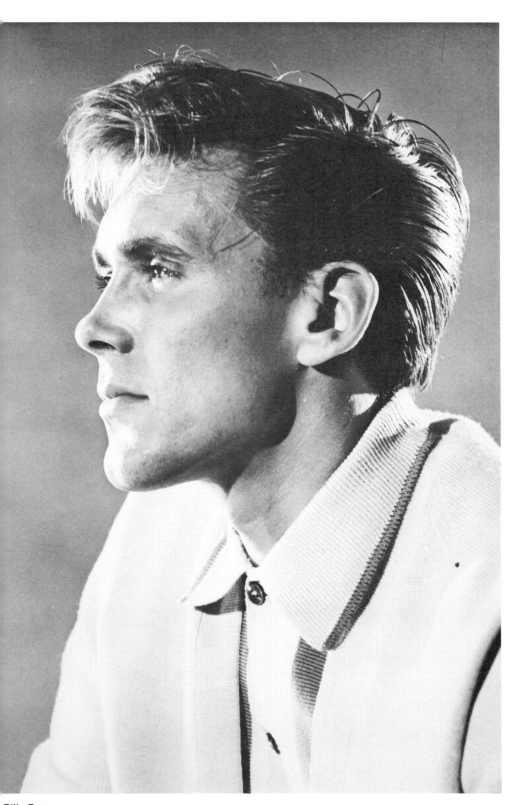

Billy Fury

1962 TOP 40

No	Title	Artist
1	Wonderful Land	Shadows
2	I Remember You	Frank Ifield
3	The Young Ones	Cliff Richard and the Shadows
4	Good Luck Charm	Elvis Presley
5	Lovesick Blues	Frank Ifield
6	Telstar	Tornados
7	Rock-A-Hula Baby/Can't Help Falling In Love	Elvis Presley
8	She's Not You	Elvis Presley
9	Return To Sender	Elvis Presley
10	I Can't Stop Loving You	Ray Charles
11	Come Outside	Mike Sarne with Wendy Richard
12	Nut Rocker	B. Bumble and the Stingers
13	Moon River	Danny Williams
14	Speedy Gonzales	Pat Boone
15	Let's Dance	Chris Montez
16	I'm Looking Out The Window/Do You Wanna Dance	Cliff Richard and the Shadows
17	Tell Me What He Said	Helen Shapiro
18	Loco-Motion	Little Eva
19	Stranger On The Shore	Mr. Acker Bilk with The Leon Young String Chorale
20	A Picture Of You	Joe Brown and the Bruvvers
21	Let's Twist Again	Chubby Checker
22	Dream Baby	Roy Orbison
23	The Next Time/Bachelor Boy	Cliff Richard and the Shadows
24	Swiss Maid	Del Shannon
25	Things	Bobby Darin
26	It'll Be Me	Cliff Richard and the Shadows
27	Hey! Baby	Bruce Channel
28	Hey Little Girl	Del Shannon
29	Midnight In Moscow	Kenny Ball and his Jazzmen
30	Forget Me Not	Eden Kane
31	Let There Be Drums	Sandy Nelson
32	Sheila	Tommy Roe
33	Happy Birthday Sweet Sixteen	Neil Sedaka
34	Roses Are Red	Ronnie Carroll
35	Bobby's Girl	Susan Maughan
36	It Might As Well Rain Until September	Carole King
37	Sun Arise	Rolf Harris
38	Sealed With A Kiss	Brian Hyland
39	Speak To Me Pretty	Brenda Lee
40	Dance On	Shadows

Elvis Presley

MERSEYSIDE'S OWN ENTERTAINMENTS PAPER

Can you give a couple
of hours per week
to
MERSEYSIDES OWN
CHARITY
THE LEAGUE OF
WELLDOERS (inc)
119-121 LIMEKILN LANE

MERSEY BEAT

There are over 1,000
Deaf or Dumb on
Merseyside
— Please Support —
LIVERPOOL ADULT
DEAF AND DUMB
BENEVOLENT
SOCIETY
ROYal 4899

VOL 1 NO 2   JULY 20—AUGUST 3   Price THREEPENCE

BEATLE'S SIGN RECORDING CONTRACT !

Left to Right
Pete Best
George Harrison
John Lennon
Paul MacArthy
Stuart Sutcliffe

BERT KAEMPFERT, who may be remembered for his golden record 'Wonderland By Night' which reached the top of the American hit parade, contracted the Beatles for Polydor, Germany's top recording company. Under the contract they will make four records per year for the company.

At a recording session, the Beatles provided vocals and backing for three numbers for Tony Sheridan. Tony, a first-class songwriter, penned 'Why', a number familiar to readers through Gerry Marsden's excellent rendering. Apart from waxing 'Why', the Beatles recorded 'My Bonny Lies Over The Ocean' opening in waltz-time, then breaking into a rock beat. Finally, the group provided good bass and drum backing to Sheridan for 'The Saints Go Marching In', a very popular number in Germany.

The Beatles recorded two further numbers for Kaempfert on their own. One side, an instrumental written by George Harrison, has not yet been named—probable titles include 'Cry For A Shadow' and 'Beatle Bop'. The other side, 'Ain't She Sweet', featured a vocal by John Lennon. The boys weren't quite satisfied with these two numbers, so they sold the rights to Polydor. Thus, in fact, under the contract the Beatles still have four more records to make this year.

Bass-guitarist Stuart Sutcliffe has remained in Hamburg and will shortly be marrying a German girl. At present he is studying at Hamburg Art College and has an English tutor. The group have no plans for taking on another guitarist, but have decided to remain a quartet.

MERSEYSIDE'S OWN ENTERTAINMENTS PAPER

WHY NOT BE A
BLOOD DONOR
NOW !

MERSEY BEAT

Please Support
LIVERPOOL ADULT
DEAF AND DUMB
BENEVOLENT SOCIETY
Parkway, Princes Ave., L'pool 8

VOL 1 NO 4   AUGUST 17 - 31, 1961   Price THREEPENCE

THE BEATLES
AGAIN !
SEEN HERE
DURING THE
RECENT
ALL-NIGHT
SESSION
AT THE
CAVERN

Photo by Dick Deck

BELOW
THE FABULOUS
MR. FARON
WITH GERRY
AND THE
PACEMAKERS

Photo by Graham

IN THIS ISSUE

FABULOUS
PHOTOGRAPHS OF
THE BEATLES
KENNY BALL
GERRY
MARSDEN
RAY WALKER
JOHNNY SANDON
RINGO STARR
GEORGE
HARRISON

THE REMO FOUR
SEE PAGE TWO

CARL VINCENT & THE COUNTS
SEE PAGE TWO

ENTERTAINMENTS GUIDE   SEE PAGE THREE

PLUS
MERSEY
ROUNDABOUT AND
OTHER REGULAR
FEATURES

1963 TOP 40

No	Title	Artist
1	From Me To You	Beatles
2	She Loves You	Beatles
3	You'll Never Walk Alone	Gerry and the Pacemakers
4	I Like It	Gerry and the Pacemakers
5	How Do You Do It	Gerry and the Pacemakers
6	The Next Time/Bachelor Boy	Cliff Richard and the Shadows
7	Summer Holiday	Cliff Richard and the Shadows
8	Do You Love Me	Brian Poole and the Tremeloes
9	Wayward Wind	Frank Ifield
10	Bad To Me	Billy J. Kramer and the Dakotas
11	Diamonds	Jet Harris and Tony Meehan
12	I Want To Hold Your Hand	Beatles
13	Confessin'	Frank Ifield
14	Sweets For My Sweet	Searchers
15	(You're The) Devil In Disguise	Elvis Presley
16	Foot Tapper	Shadows
17	Dance On	Shadows
18	From A Jack To A King	Ned Miller
19	Please Please Me	Beatles
20	It's All In The Game	Cliff Richard
21	Do You Want To Know A Secret	Billy J. Kramer and the Dakotas
22	Atlantis	Shadows
23	Then He Kissed Me	Crystals
24	I'm Telling You Now	Freddie and the Dreamers
25	Return to Sender	Elvis Presley
26	Scarlett O'Hara	Jet Harris and Tony Meehan
27	Sugar And Spice	Searchers
28	Don't Talk To Him	Cliff Richard
29	Can't Get Used To Losing You	Andy Williams
30	You Were Made For Me	Freddie and the Dreamers
31	If You Gotta Make A Fool Of Somebody	Freddie and the Dreamers
32	Like I Do	Maureen Evans
33	That's What Love Will Do	Joe Brown and the Bruvvers
34	Blue Bayou/Mean Woman Blues	Roy Orbison
35	Like I've Never Been Gone	Billy Fury
36	The Night Has A Thousand Eyes	Bobby Vee
37	When Will You Say I Love You	Billy Fury
38	Lovesick Blues	Frank Ifield
39	I Want To Stay Here	Steve and Eydie
40	Brown-Eyed Handsome Man	Buddy Holly

1964 TOP 40

No	Title	Artist
1	You're My World	Cilla Black
2	I Feel Fine	Beatles
3	Oh Pretty Woman	Roy Orbison
4	A Hard Day's Night	Beatles
5	Anyone Who Had A Heart	Cilla Black
6	Can't Buy Me Love	Beatles
7	(There's) Always Something There To Remind Me	Sandie Shaw
8	Needles And Pins	Searchers
9	It's Over	Roy Orbison
10	Glad All Over	Dave Clark Five
11	Have I The Right	Honeycombs
12	Little Children	Billy J. Kramer and the Dakotas
13	I'm Into Something Good	Herman's Hermits
14	Do Wah Diddy Diddy	Manfred Mann
15	Don't Throw Your Love Away	Searchers
16	I Want To Hold Your Hand	Beatles
17	A World Without Love	Peter and Gordon
18	You Really Got Me	Kinks
19	Baby Love	Supremes
20	It's All Over Now	Rolling Stones
21	Juliet	Four Pennies
22	Diane	Bachelors
23	House Of The Rising Sun	Animals
24	Little Red Rooster	Rolling Stones
25	Downtown	Petula Clark
26	Bits And Pieces	Dave Clark Five
27	I'm Gonna Be Strong	Gene Pitney
28	Someone Someone	Brian Poole and the Tremeloes
29	I'm The One	Gerry and the Pacemakers
30	Rag Doll	Four Seasons
31	All Day And All Of The Night	Kinks
32	I Believe	Bachelors
33	Hippy Hippy Shake	Swinging Blue Jeans
34	My Boy Lollipop	Millie
35	Just One Look	Hollies
36	I Won't Forget You	Jim Reeves
37	Where Did Our Love Go	Supremes
38	The Wedding	Julie Rogers
39	Call Up The Groups	Barron Knights
40	I Just Don't Know What To Do With Myself	Dusty Springfield

1965 TOP 40

No	Title	Artist
1	Tears	Ken Dodd
2	The Carnival Is Over	Seekers
3	Help	Beatles
4	Ticket To Ride	Beatles
5	I'm Alive	Hollies
6	The Last Time	Rolling Stones
7	Day Tripper/We Can Work It Out	Beatles
8	Get Off Of My Cloud	Rolling Stones
9	Long Live Love	Sandie Shaw
10	Crying In The Chapel	Elvis Presley
11	I Got You Babe	Sonny and Cher
12	I'll Never Find Another You	Seekers
13	(I Can't Get No) Satisfaction	Rolling Stones
14	Mr. Tambourine Man	Byrds
15	Yeh Yeh	Georgie Fame and the Blue Flames
16	You've Lost That Lovin' Feeling	Righteous Brothers
17	It's Not Unusual	Tom Jones
18	Concrete And Clay	Unit Four Plus Two
19	Tired Of Waiting For You	Kinks
20	Where Are You Now (My Love)	Jackie Trent
21	Make It Easy On Yourself	Walker Brothers
22	Go Now	Moody Blues
23	The Minute You're Gone	Cliff Richard
24	King Of The Road	Roger Miller
25	I Feel Fine	Beatles
26	Heart Full Of Soul	Yardbirds
27	Almost There	Andy Williams
28	Wind Me Up (Let Me Go)	Cliff Richard
29	My Generation	Who
30	You've Got Your Troubles	Fortunes
31	The Price Of Love	Everly Brothers
32	Here Comes The Night	Them
33	If You Gotta Go Go Now	Manfred Mann
34	True Love Ways	Peter and Gordon
35	We've Gotta Get Out Of This Place	Animals
36	Game Of Love	Wayne Fontana and the Mindbenders
37	You've Lost That Lovin' Feeling	Cilla Black
38	A World Of Our Own	Seekers
39	Silhouettes	Herman's Hermits
40	Yesterday Man	Chris Andrews

Four Tops

1966 TOP 40

No	Title	Artist
1	Distant Drums	Jim Reeves
2	Green Green Grass Of Home	Tom Jones
3	The Sun Ain't Gonna Shine Anymore	Walker Brothers
4	Yellow Submarine/Eleanor Rigby	Beatles
5	These Boots Are Made For Walkin'	Nancy Sinatra
6	Strangers In The Night	Frank Sinatra
7	Reach Out I'll Be There	Four Tops
8	Pretty Flamingo	Manfred Mann
9	Michelle	Overlanders
10	Good Vibrations	Beach Boys
11	Paperback Writer	Beatles
12	With A Girl Like You	Troggs
13	Sunny Afternoon	Kinks
14	Somebody Help Me	Spencer Davis Group
15	Day Tripper/We Can Work It Out	Beatles
16	Keep On Running	Spencer Davis Group
17	All Or Nothing	Small Faces
18	Out Of Time	Chris Farlowe
19	Paint It Black	Rolling Stones
20	You Don't Have To Say You Love Me	Dusty Springfield
21	Get Away	Georgie Fame and the Blue Flames
22	I Can't Let Go	Hollies
23	Nineteenth Nervous Breakdown	Rolling Stones
24	God Only Knows	Beach Boys
25	Bend It	Dave Dee, Dozy, Beaky, Mick and Tich
26	Daydream	Lovin' Spoonful
27	Morningtown Ride	Seekers
28	Stop Stop Stop	Hollies
29	What Would I Be	Val Doonican
30	I'm A Boy	Who
31	A Groovy Kind Of Love	Mindbenders
32	Wild Thing	Troggs
33	Black Is Black	Los Bravos
34	You Were On My Mind	Crispian St. Peters
35	Gimme Some Lovin'	Spencer Davis Group
36	I Can't Control Myself	Troggs
37	Semi-Detached Suburban Mr. James	Manfred Mann
38	Wind Me Up (Let Me Go)	Cliff Richard
39	Sloop John B.	Beach Boys
40	Nobody Needs Your Love	Gene Pitney

1967 TOP 40

No	Title	Artist
1	Release Me	Engelbert Humperdinck
2	A Whiter Shade Of Pale	Procol Harum
3	The Last Waltz	Engelbert Humperdinck
4	Massachusetts	Bee Gees
5	San Francisco (Be Sure To Wear Flowers In Your Hair)	Scott McKenzie
6	I'm A Believer	Monkees
7	Hello Goodbye	Beatles
8	All You Need Is Love	Beatles
9	Puppet On A String	Sandie Shaw
10	Silence Is Golden	Tremeloes
11	Somethin' Stupid	Nancy Sinatra and Frank Sinatra
12	Baby Now That I've Found You	Foundations
13	Let The Heartaches Begin	Long John Baldry
14	Green Green Grass Of Home	Tom Jones
15	This Is My Song	Petula Clark
16	I'll Never Fall In Love Again	Tom Jones
17	There Goes My Everything	Engelbert Humperdinck
18	Penny Lane/Strawberry Fields Forever	Beatles
19	Waterloo Sunset	Kinks
20	Everybody Knows	Dave Clark Five
21	Flowers In The Rain	Move
22	Matthew And Son	Cat Stevens
23	Excerpt From 'A Teenage Opera'	Keith West
24	Morningtown Ride	Seekers
25	Dedicated To The One I Love	Mamas and Papas
26	Alternate Title	Monkees
27	Hole In My Shoe	Traffic
28	It Must Be Him (Seul Sur Son Etoile)	Vikki Carr
29	Edelweiss	Vince Hill
30	Night Of Fear	Move
31	This Is My Song	Harry Secombe
32	I'm Coming Home	Tom Jones
33	Sunshine Superman	Donovan
34	Magical Mystery Tour (Double EP)	Beatles
35	A Little Bit Me, A Little Bit You	Monkees
36	Let's Spend The Night Together	Rolling Stones
37	Zabadak!	Dave Dee, Dozy, Beaky, Mick and Tich
38	Death Of A Clown	Dave Davies
39	Carrie Anne	Hollies
40	If The Whole World Stopped Loving	Val Doonican

Sandie Shaw and Tom Jones

1968 TOP 40

No	Title	Artist
1	Those Were The Days	Mary Hopkin
2	Young Girl	Union Gap featuring Gary Puckett
3	The Good, The Bad And The Ugly	Hugo Montenegro
4	What A Wonderful World/Cabaret	Louis Armstrong
5	Mony Mony	Tommy James and the Shondells
6	Cinderella Rockefella	Esther and Abi Ofarim
7	Lily the Pink	Scaffold
8	Baby Come Back	Equals
9	Hello Goodbye	Beatles
10	Hey Jude	Beatles
11	Everlasting Love	Love Affair
12	Mighty Quinn	Manfred Mann
13	Jumping Jack Flash	Rolling Stones
14	Congratulations	Cliff Richard
15	Lady Madonna	Beatles
16	I Gotta Get A Message To You	Bee Gees
17	Legend Of Xanadu	Dave Dee, Dozy, Beaky, Mick and Tich
18	Fire	Crazy World of Arthur Brown
19	Ballad Of Bonnie And Clyde	Georgie Fame
20	With A Little Help From My Friends	Joe Cocker
21	I Pretend	Des O'Connor
22	Do It Again	Beach Boys
23	A Man Without Love	Engelbert Humperdinck
24	Delilah	Tom Jones
25	Son Of Hickory Holler's Tramp	O. C. Smith
26	Eloise	Barry Ryan
27	Magical Mystery Tour (Double EP)	Beatles
28	Jesamine	Casuals
29	Honey	Bobby Goldsboro
30	Simon Says	1910 Fruitgum Co.
31	Ain't Got No—I Got Life/Do What You Gotta Do	Nina Simone
32	Lazy Sunday	Small Faces
33	Build Me Up Buttercup	Foundations
34	Little Arrows	Leapy Lee
35	This Guy's In Love With You	Herb Alpert
36	This Old Heart Of Mine	Isley Brothers
37	Am I That Easy To Forget	Engelbert Humperdinck
38	If I Only Had Time	John Rowles
39	Judy In Disguise (With Glasses)	John Fred and the Playboy Band
40	Bend Me Shape Me	Amen Corner

Rolling Stones

1969 TOP 40

No	Title	Artist
1	Sugar Sugar	Archies
2	Get Back	Beatles with Billy Preston
3	Honky Tonk Woman	Rolling Stones
4	Where Do You Go To My Lovely	Peter Sarstedt
5	I Heard It Through The Grapevine	Marvin Gaye
6	Bad Moon Rising	Creedence Clearwater Revival
7	The Ballad Of John And Yoko	Beatles
8	In The Year 2525 (Exordium And Terminus)	Zager and Evans
9	Ob-La-Di Ob-La-Da	Marmalade
10	Something In The Air	Thunderclap Newman
11	(If Paradise Is) Half As Nice	Amen Corner
12	Two Little Boys	Rolf Harris
13	Albatross	Fleetwood Mac
14	I'll Never Fall In Love Again	Bobbie Gentry
15	Je T'Aime ... Moi Non Plus	Jane Birkin and Serge Gainsbourg
16	Dizzy	Tommy Roe
17	The Israelites	Desmond Dekker and the Aces
18	Blackberry Way	Move
19	Lily The Pink	Scaffold
20	Goodbye	Mary Hopkin
21	Ruby Don't Take Your Love To Town	Kenny Rogers and the First Edition
22	In The Ghetto	Elvis Presley
23	Give Peace A Chance	John Lennon/Plastic Ono Band
24	Saved By The Bell	Robin Gibb
25	Oh Well	Fleetwood Mac
26	(Call Me) Number One	Tremeloes
27	Oh Happy Day	Edwin Hawkins Singers
28	My Sentimental Friend	Herman's Hermits
29	Man Of The World	Fleetwood Mac
30	I'm Gonna Make You Mine	Lou Christie
31	Don't Forget To Remember	Bee Gees
32	Yester-Me Yester-You Yesterday	Stevie Wonder
33	Build Me Up Buttercup	Foundations
34	Gentle On My Mind	Dean Martin
35	Boom Bang-A-Bang	Lulu
36	For Once In My Life	Stevie Wonder
37	The Way It Used To Be	Engelbert Humperdinck
38	I'm Gonna Make You Love Me	Diana Ross and the Supremes and the Temptations
39	Please Don't Go	Donald Peers
40	He Ain't Heavy He's My Brother	Hollies

Fleetwood Mac

1970 TOP 40

No	Title	Artist
1	In The Summertime	Mungo Jerry
2	The Wonder Of You	Elvis Presley
3	Band Of Gold	Freda Payne
4	Love Grows (Where My Rosemary Goes)	Edison Lighthouse
5	I Hear You Knockin'	Dave Edmunds
6	Two Little Boys	Rolf Harris
7	Bridge Over Troubled Water	Simon and Garfunkel
8	Back Home	England World Cup Squad
9	Wand'rin' Star	Lee Marvin
10	Woodstock	Matthews Southern Comfort
11	Spirit In The Sky	Norman Greenbaum
12	All Kinds Of Everything	Dana
13	Tears Of A Clown	Smokey Robinson and the Miracles
14	Yellow River	Christie
15	Voodoo Chile	Jimi Hendrix Experience
16	All Right Now	Free
17	Patches	Clarence Carter
18	Ruby Don't Take Your Love To Town	Kenny Rogers and the First Edition
19	When I'm Dead And Gone	McGuinness Flint
20	Black Night	Deep Purple
21	Neanderthal Man	Hotlegs
22	You Can Get It If You Really Want	Desmond Dekker
23	Groovin' With Mr. Bloe	Mr. Bloe
24	Let's Work Together	Canned Heat
25	Lola	Kinks
26	Question	Moody Blues
27	Leavin' On A Jet Plane	Peter, Paul and Mary
28	Let It Be	Beatles
29	I Want You Back	Jackson Five
30	Knock Knock Who's There	Mary Hopkin
31	Suspicious Minds	Elvis Presley
32	Can't Help Falling In Love	Andy Williams
33	Cracklin' Rosie	Neil Diamond
34	Reflections Of My Life	Marmalade
35	Indian Reservation	Don Fardon
36	Give Me Just A Little More Time	Chairmen Of The Board
37	Mama Told Me Not To Come	Three Dog Night
38	Rainbow	Marmalade
39	All I Have To Do Is Dream	Bobbie Gentry and Glen Campbell
40	Up Around The Bend	Creedence Clearwater Revival

1971 TOP 40

No	Title	Artist
1	Hot Love	T. Rex
2	Maggie May	Rod Stewart
3	Knock Three Times	Dawn
4	Chirpy Chirpy Cheep Cheep	Middle Of The Road
5	My Sweet Lord	George Harrison
6	I'm Still Waiting	Diana Ross
7	Coz I Luv You	Slade
8	Get It On	T. Rex
9	Hey Girl Don't Bother Me	Tams
10	Grandad	Clive Dunn
11	Ernie (The Fastest Milkman In The West)	Benny Hill
12	Double Barrel	Dave and Ansil Collins
13	Baby Jump	Mungo Jerry
14	I Hear You Knockin'	Dave Edmunds
15	Never Ending Song Of Love	New Seekers
16	Pushbike Song	Mixtures
17	Jeepster	T. Rex
18	Brown Sugar/Bitch/Let It Rock	Rolling Stones
19	Bridget The Midget	Ray Stevens
20	Witch Queen Of New Orleans	Redbone
21	Co Co	Sweet
22	Another Day	Paul McCartney
23	I Did What I Did For Maria	Tony Christie
24	Did You Ever	Nancy and Lee
25	Indiana Wants Me	R. Dean Taylor
26	Tweedle Dee Tweedle Dum	Middle Of The Road
27	Don't Let It Die	Hurricane Smith
28	Ride A White Swan	T. Rex
29	Till	Tom Jones
30	Rose Garden	Lynn Anderson
31	When I'm Dead And Gone	McGuinness Flint
32	Banner Man	Blue Mink
33	Stoned Love	Supremes
34	Resurrection Shuffle	Ashton, Gardner and Dyke
35	What Are You Doing Sunday	Dawn
36	Simple Game	Four Tops
37	Johnny Reggae	Piglets
38	Heaven Must Have Sent You	Elgins
39	It Don't Come Easy	Ringo Starr
40	Devil's Answer	Atomic Rooster

1972   TOP 40

No	Title	Artist
1	Without You	Nilsson
2	Amazing Grace	The Pipes and Drums and Military Band of the Royal Scots Dragoon Guards
3	Puppy Love	Donny Osmond
4	My Ding-A-Ling	Chuck Berry
5	Mouldy Old Dough	Lieutenant Pigeon
6	I'd Like To Teach The World To Sing	New Seekers
7	Metal Guru	T. Rex
8	Son Of My Father	Chicory Tip
9	School's Out	Alice Cooper
10	Mama Weer All Crazee Now	Slade
11	Telegram Sam	T. Rex
12	Vincent	Don McLean
13	How Can I Be Sure	David Cassidy
14	Clair	Gilbert O'Sullivan
15	Long Haired Lover From Liverpool	Little Jimmy Osmond
16	You Wear It Well	Rod Stewart
17	Take Me Bak 'Ome	Slade
18	Ernie (The Fastest Milkman In The West)	Benny Hill
19	American Pie	Don McLean
20	Beg Steal Or Borrow	New Seekers
21	Mother Of Mine	Neil Reid
22	Crazy Horses	Osmonds
23	Rock 'n' Roll Parts 1 & 2	Gary Glitter
24	Children Of The Revolution	T. Rex
25	Donna	10 C.C.
26	Back Off Boogaloo	Ringo Starr
27	Seaside Shuffle	Terry Dactyl and the Dinosaurs
28	Sylvia's Mother	Dr. Hook and the Medicine Show
29	Could It Be Forever/Cherish	David Cassidy
30	Come What May	Vicky Leandros
31	Gudbuy T'Jane	Slade
32	Jeepster	T. Rex
33	Rocket Man	Elton John
34	Silver Machine	Hawkwind
35	Solid Gold Easy Action	T. Rex
36	You're A Lady	Peter Skellern
37	Alone Again (Naturally)	Gilbert O'Sullivan
38	A Horse With No Name	America
39	Breaking Up Is Hard To Do	Partridge Family
40	At The Club/Saturday Night At The Movies	Drifters

Donny Osmond

1973 TOP 40

No	Title	Artist
1	Blockbuster	Sweet
2	I Love You Love Me Love	Gary Glitter
3	Eye Level	Simon Park Orchestra
4	Tie A Yellow Ribbon Round The Old Oak Tree	Dawn
5	I'm The Leader Of The Gang (I Am)	Gary Glitter
6	Cum On Feel The Noize	Slade
7	See My Baby Jive	Wizzard
8	Young Love	Donny Osmond
9	Daydreamer/The Puppy Song	David Cassidy
10	Long Haired Lover From Liverpool	Little Jimmy Osmond
11	Skweeze Me Pleeze Me	Slade
12	Merry Xmas Everybody	Slade
13	Get Down	Gilbert O'Sullivan
14	Welcome Home	Peters and Lee
15	The Twelfth Of Never	Donny Osmond
16	Rubber Bullets	10 C.C.
17	Can The Can	Suzi Quatro
18	Angel Fingers	Wizzard
19	Hello Hello I'm Back Again	Gary Glitter
20	Part Of The Union	Strawbs
21	Ballroom Blitz	Sweet
22	Hell Raiser	Sweet
23	Let Me In	Osmonds
24	Do You Wanna Touch Me	Gary Glitter
25	Yesterday Once More	Carpenters
26	(Dancing) On A Saturday Night	Barry Blue
27	Jean Genie	David Bowie
28	My Frend Stan	Slade
29	Paper Roses	Marie Osmond
30	My Coo-Ca-Choo	Alvin Stardust
31	Albatross	Fleetwood Mac
32	Solid Gold Easy Action	T. Rex
33	Cindy Incidentally	Faces
34	Life On Mars	David Bowie
35	You Won't Find Another Fool Like Me	New Seekers
36	20th Century Boy	T. Rex
37	Sorrow	David Bowie
38	And I Love You So	Perry Como
39	Alright Alright Alright	Mungo Jerry
40	Rock On	David Essex

Sweet

1974 TOP 40

No	Title	Artist
1	She	Charles Aznavour
2	Tiger Feet	Mud
3	Sugar Baby Love	Rubettes
4	Seasons In The Sun	Terry Jacks
5	Gonna Make You A Star	David Essex
6	Billy Don't Be A Hero	Paper Lace
7	Rock Your Baby	George McCrae
8	Everything I Own	Ken Boothe
9	Kung Fu Fighting	Carl Douglas
10	Love Me For A Reason	Osmonds
11	When Will I See You Again	Three Degrees
12	Devil Gate Drive	Suzi Quatro
13	Waterloo	Abba
14	You're The First The Last My Everything	Barry White
15	Merry Xmas Everybody	Slade
16	Lonely This Christmas	Mud
17	Annie's Song	John Denver
18	You Won't Find Another Fool Like Me	Seekers
19	Jealous Mind	Alvin Stardust
20	The Streak	Ray Stevens
21	Always Yours	Gary Glitter
22	Sad Sweet Dreamer	Sweet Sensation
23	Kissin' In The Back Row Of The Movies	Drifters
24	Teenage Rampage	Sweet
25	This Town Ain't Big Enough For The Both Of Us	Sparks
26	Killer Queen	Queen
27	You Ain't Seen Nothing Yet	Bachman-Turner Overdrive
28	Far Far Away	Slade
29	The Cat Crept In	Mud
30	The Air That I Breathe	Hollies
31	Hey Rock And Roll	Showaddywaddy
32	You Make Me Feel Brand New	Stylistics
33	The Show Must Go On	Leo Sayer
34	Born With A Smile On My Face	Stephanie De Sykes and Rain
35	I'm Leaving It (All) Up To You	Donny and Marie Osmond
36	The Most Beautiful Girl	Charlie Rich
37	Oh Yes! You're Beautiful	Gary Glitter
38	Shang-A-Lang	Bay City Rollers
39	Rock Me Gently	Andy Kim
40	Juke Box Jive	Rubettes

1975 TOP 40

No	Title	Artist
1	Bye Bye Baby	Bay City Rollers
2	Bohemian Rhapsody	Queen
3	Sailing	Rod Stewart
4	Whispering Grass	Windsor Davies and Don Estelle
5	Hold Me Close	David Essex
6	I Can't Give You Anything (But My Love)	Stylistics
7	Stand By Your Man	Tammy Wynette
8	Give A Little Love	Bay City Rollers
9	January	Pilot
10	I Only Have Eyes For You	Art Garfunkel
11	Space Oddity	David Bowie
12	If	Telly Savalas
13	I'm Not In Love	10 C.C.
14	Oh Boy	Mud
15	Make Me Smile (Come Up And See Me)	Steve Harley and Cockney Rebel
16	Lonely This Christmas	Mud
17	Barbados	Typically Tropical
18	Tears On My Pillow	Johnny Nash
19	D.I.V.O.R.C.E.	Billy Connolly
20	Ms Grace	Tymes
21	Down Down	Status Quo
22	You Sexy Thing	Hot Chocolate
23	There's A Whole Lot Of Loving	Guys and Dolls
24	Loving You	Minnie Riperton
25	Fox On The Run	Sweet
26	The Trail Of The Lonesome Pine	Laurel and Hardy with the Avalon Boys
27	The Streets Of London	Ralph McTell
28	The Last Farewell	Roger Whittaker
29	Three Steps To Heaven	Showaddywaddy
30	Please Mr. Postman	Carpenters
31	Misty	Ray Stevens
32	Love Is The Drug	Roxy Music
33	Moonlighting	Leo Sayer
34	Honey	Bobby Goldsboro
35	Never Can Say Goodbye	Gloria Gaynor
36	Goodbye My Love	Glitter Band
37	Wombling Merry Christmas	Wombles
38	There Goes My First Love	Drifters
39	The Bump	Kenny
40	The Hustle	Van McCoy

1976 TOP 40

No	Title	Artist
1	Save Your Kisses For Me	Brotherhood Of Man
2	Don't Go Breaking My Heart	Elton John and Kiki Dee
3	Dancing Queen	Abba
4	Fernando	Abba
5	Mississippi	Pussycat
6	Bohemian Rhapsody	Queen
7	If You Leave Me Now	Chicago
8	Under The Moon Of Love	Showaddywaddy
9	I Love To Love (But My Baby Loves To Dance)	Tina Charles
10	You To Me Are Everything	Real Thing
11	December '63 (Oh What A Night)	Four Seasons
12	Combine Harvester (Brand New Key)	Wurzels
13	Mamma Mia	Abba
14	Forever And Ever	Slik
15	No Charge	J. J. Barrie
16	When A Child Is Born (Soleado)	Johnny Mathis
17	The Roussos Phenomenon (EP)	Demis Roussos
18	A Little Bit More	Dr. Hook
19	Let 'Em In	Wings
20	Can't Get By Without You	Real Thing
21	When Forever Has Gone	Demis Roussos
22	You See The Trouble With Me	Barry White
23	Glass Of Champagne	Sailor
24	You Make Me Feel Like Dancing	Leo Sayer
25	Love Really Hurts Without You	Billy Ocean
26	Convoy	C. W. McCall
27	Silly Love Songs	Wings
28	Somebody To Love	Queen
29	Young Hearts Run Free	Candi Staton
30	The Trail Of The Lonesome Pine	Laurel and Hardy with the Avalon Boys
31	I Believe In Father Christmas	Greg Lake
32	You Just Might See Me Cry	Our Kid
33	The Killing Of Georgie	Rod Stewart
34	Jungle Rock	Hank Mizell
35	Jeans On	David Dundas
36	Music	John Miles
37	Sailing	Rod Stewart
38	Money Money Money	Abba
39	Love Machine	Miracles
40	Rodrigo's Guitar Concerto De Aranjuez	Manuel and his Music Of The Mountains

Elton John and Kiki Dee

1977 TOP 40

No	Title	Artist
1	Knowing Me Knowing You	Abba
2	Way Down	Elvis Presley
3	Mull Of Kintyre/Girls' School	Wings
4	I Don't Want To Talk About It/First Cut Is The Deepest	Rod Stewart
5	Don't Give Up On Us	David Soul
6	I Feel Love	Donna Summer
7	The Name Of The Game	Abba
8	Silver Lady	David Soul
9	So You Win Again	Hot Chocolate
10	When I Need You	Leo Sayer
11	Chanson D'Amour	Manhattan Transfer
12	Free	Deniece Williams
13	When A Child Is Born (Soleado)	Johnny Mathis
14	Don't Cry For Me Argentina	Julie Covington
15	Angelo	Brotherhood Of Man
16	Yes Sir I Can Boogie	Baccara
17	Lucille	Kenny Rogers
18	Show You The Way To Go	Jacksons
19	Float On	Floaters
20	The Floral Dance	Brighouse and Rastrick Brass Band
21	Black Is Black	La Belle Epoque
22	Magic Fly	Space
23	Going In With My Eyes Open	David Soul
24	We Are The Champions	Queen
25	Red Light Spells Danger	Billy Ocean
26	Under The Moon Of Love	Showaddywaddy
27	Fanfare For The Common Man	Emerson, Lake and Palmer
28	Ma Baker	Boney M
29	Ain't Gonna Bump No More (With No Big Fat Woman)	Joe Tex
30	Boogie Nights	Heatwave
31	You Got What It Takes	Showaddywaddy
32	Sir Duke	Stevie Wonder
33	God Save The Queen	Sex Pistols
34	How Deep Is Your Love	Bee Gees
35	Side Show	Barry Biggs
36	Rockin' All Over The World	Status Quo
37	You're In My Heart	Rod Stewart
38	Money Money Money	Abba
39	Love Theme From A Star Is Born (Evergreen)	Barbra Streisand
40	When	Showaddywaddy

1978 TOP 40

No	Title	Artist
1	You're The One That I Want	John Travolta and Olivia Newton-John
2	Summer Nights	John Travolta and Olivia Newton-John
3	Rivers Of Babylon/Brown Girl In The Ring	Boney M
4	Three Times A Lady	Commodores
5	Mull Of Kintyre/Girls' School	Wings
6	Wuthering Heights	Kate Bush
7	Mary's Boy Child/Oh My Lord	Boney M
8	Take A Chance On Me	Abba
9	Matchstalk Men And Matchstalk Cats And Dogs	Brian and Michael
10	Night Fever	Bee Gees
11	Rat Trap	Boomtown Rats
12	Figaro	Brotherhood Of Man
13	Uptown Top Ranking	Althia and Donna
14	Dreadlock Holiday	10 C.C.
15	Da Ya Think I'm Sexy	Rod Stewart
16	The Smurf Song	Father Abraham and the Smurfs
17	Denis	Blondie
18	Y.M.C.A.	Village People
19	Substitute	Clout
20	Rasputin	Boney M
21	Hopelessly Devoted To You	Olivia Newton-John
22	Love Don't Live Here Anymore	Rose Royce
23	The Floral Dance	Brighouse and Rastrick Brass Band
24	Boy From New York City	Darts
25	Come Back My Love	Darts
26	Sandy	John Travolta
27	It's Raining	Darts
28	I Wonder Why	Showaddywaddy
29	Love's Unkind	Donna Summer
30	Baker Street	Gerry Rafferty
31	Dancing In The City	Marshall Hain
32	A Taste Of Aggro	Barron Knights
33	Annie's Song	James Galway
34	Grease	Frankie Valli
35	Wishing On A Star	Rose Royce
36	Too Much Too Little Too Late	Johnny Mathis and Deniece Williams
37	If I Had Words	Scott Fitzgerald and Yvonne Keeley
38	Too Much Heaven	Bee Gees
39	Lucky Stars	Dean Friedman
40	Miss You	Rolling Stones

Cliff Richard

1979 TOP 40

No	Title	Artist
1	Bright Eyes	Art Garfunkel
2	We Don't Talk Anymore	Cliff Richard
3	Are 'Friends' Electric	Tubeway Army
4	I Don't Like Mondays	Boomtown Rats
5	Heart Of Glass	Blondie
6	I Will Survive	Gloria Gaynor
7	When You're In Love With A Beautiful Woman	Dr. Hook
8	Y.M.C.A.	Village People
9	Sunday Girl	Blondie
10	One Day At A Time	Lena Martell
11	Message In A Bottle	Police
12	Another Brick In The Wall (Part II)	Pink Floyd
13	Ring My Bell	Anita Ward
14	Tragedy	Bee Gees
15	Hit Me With Your Rhythm Stick	Ian and the Blockheads
16	Cars	Gary Numan
17	Video Killed The Radio Star	Buggles
18	Walking On The Moon	Police
19	Dance Away	Roxy Music
20	Oliver's Army	Elvis Costello and the Attractions
21	Some Girls	Racey
22	Pop Muzik	M
23	Silly Games	Janet Kay
24	Crazy Little Thing Called Love	Queen
25	Chiquitita	Abba
26	In The Navy	Village People
27	I Have A Dream	Abba
28	Bang Bang	B. A. Robertson
29	Cool For Cats	Squeeze
30	Up The Junction	Squeeze
31	Dreaming	Blondie
32	Can't Stand Losing You	Police
33	Mary's Boy Child–Oh My Lord	Boney M
34	Woman In Love	Three Degrees
35	Lay Your Love On Me	Racey
36	Hooray Hooray It's A Holi-Holiday	Boney M
37	No More Tears (Enough Is Enough)	Donna Summer and Barbra Streisand
38	C'mon Everybody	Sex Pistols
39	Lucky Number	Lene Lovich
40	Don't Stop Till You Get Enough	Michael Jackson

1980 TOP 40

No	Title	Artist
1	Don't Stand So Close To Me	Police
2	Woman In Love	Barbra Streisand
3	Crying	Don McLean
4	Super Trouper	Abba
5	Theme From M*A*S*H (Suicide Is Painless)	Mash
6	Going Underground/Dreams Of Children	Jam
7	Use It Up And Wear It Out	Odyssey
8	The Tide Is High	Blondie
9	Geno	Dexy's Midnight Runners
10	Coward Of The County	Kenny Rogers
11	Ashes To Ashes	David Bowie
12	Xanadu	Olivia Newton-John and the Electric Light Orchestra
13	Brass In Pocket	Pretenders
14	Atomic	Blondie
15	What's Another Year	Johnny Logan
16	The Winner Takes It All	Abba
17	Too Much Too Young (EP)	Special AKA featuring Rico
18	Working My Way Back To You/Forgive Me Girl	Detroit Spinners
19	Feels Like I'm In Love	Kelly Marie
20	Another Brick In The Wall (Part II)	Pink Floyd
21	Together We Are Beautiful	Fern Kinney
22	Start	Jam
23	There's No One Quite Like Grandma	St. Winifred's School Choir
24	Call Me	Blondie
25	(Just Like) Starting Over	John Lennon
26	D.I.S.C.O.	Ottowan
27	No Doubt About It	Hot Chocolate
28	Funky Town	Lipps Inc.
29	Dance Yourself Dizzy	Liquid Gold
30	Upside Down	Diana Ross
31	What You're Proposin'	Status Quo
32	One Day I'll Fly Away	Randy Crawford
33	With You I'm Born Again	Billy Preston and Syreeta
34	I Have A Dream	Abba
35	Coming Up	Paul McCartney
36	Masterblaster (Jammin')	Stevie Wonder
37	More Than I Can Say	Leo Sayer
38	And The Beat Goes On	Whispers
39	Take That Look Off Your Face	Marti Webb
40	Stop The Cavalry	Jona Lewie

Blondie

1981 TOP 40

No	Title	Artist
1	Stand And Deliver	Adam and the Ants
2	Prince Charming	Adam and the Ants
3	Imagine	John Lennon
4	Green Door	Shakin' Stevens
5	It's My Party	Dave Stewart with Barbara Gaskin
6	This Ole House	Shakin' Stevens
7	Ghost Town	Specials
8	Making Your Mind Up	Bucks Fizz
9	Shaddup You Face	Joe Dolce Music Theatre
10	Don't You Want Me	Human League
11	Tainted Love	Soft Cell
12	One Day In Your Life	Michael Jackson
13	Woman	John Lennon
14	Being With You	Smokey Robinson
15	Under Pressure	Queen and David Bowie
16	Jealous Guy	Roxy Music
17	Begin The Beguine (Volver A Empezar)	Julio Iglesias
18	Japanese Boy	Aneka
19	Every Little Thing She Does Is Magic	Police
20	There's No One Quite Like Grandma	St. Winifred's School Choir
21	Vienna	Ultravox
22	You Drive Me Crazy	Shakin' Stevens
23	Happy Birthday	Altered Images
24	Daddy's Home	Cliff Richard
25	Hooked On Classics	Royal Philharmonic Orchestra Cond. Louis Clark
26	Chi Mai (Theme from the TV Series *The Life And Times Of David Lloyd George*)	Ennio Morricone
27	Kids In America	Kim Wilde
28	Birdie Song (Birdie Dance)	Tweets
29	Antmusic	Adam and the Ants
30	Stars On 45 Vol. 2	Starsound
31	Stars on 45	Starsound
32	More Than In Love	Kate Robbins and Beyond
33	In The Air Tonight	Phil Collins
34	Happy Birthday	Stevie Wonder
35	Happy Xmas (War Is Over)	John Lennon
36	Invisible Sun	Police
37	O Superman	Laurie Anderson
38	Kings Of The Wild Frontier	Adam and the Ants
39	(Just Like) Starting Over	John Lennon
40	Can Can	Bad Manners

Adam and the Ants

Boy George

1982 TOP 40

No	Title	Artist
1	Come On Eileen	Dexys Midnight Runners
2	Eye Of The Tiger	Survivor
3	Fame	Irene Cara
4	The Lion Sleeps Tonight	Tight Fit
5	Do You Really Want To Hurt Me	Culture Club
6	Ebony And Ivory	Paul McCartney/Stevie Wonder
7	I Don't Wanna Dance	Eddy Grant
8	Seven Tears	Goombay Dance Band
9	Pass The Dutchie	Musical Youth
10	Town Called Malice/Precious	Jam
11	Goody Two Shoes	Adam Ant
12	The Land Of Make Believe	Bucks Fizz
13	House Of Fun	Madness
14	Don't You Want Me	Human League
15	Beat Surrender	Jam
16	Save Your Love	Renée and Renato
17	Happy Talk	Captain Sensible
18	A Little Peace	Nicole
19	My Camera Never Lies	Bucks Fizz
20	Oh Julie	Shakin' Stevens
21	The Model/Computer Love	Kraftwerk
22	I've Never Been To Me	Charlene
23	Mirror Man	Human League
24	Golden Brown	Stranglers
25	Abracadabra	Steve Miller Band
26	Heartbreaker	Dionne Warwick
27	Mickey	Toni Basil
28	The Bitterest Pill (I Ever Had To Swallow)	Jam
29	Torch	Soft Cell
30	Zoom	Fat Larry's Band
31	Save A Prayer	Duran Duran
32	Only You	Yazoo
33	Just An Illusion	Imagination
34	Private Investigations	Dire Straits
35	Ain't No Pleasing You	Chas and Dave
36	This Time (We'll Get It Right)/England We'll Fly The Flag	England World Cup Squad
37	The Shakin' Stevens EP	Shakin' Stevens
38	Da Da Da	Trio
39	One Step Further	Bardo
40	Annie, I'm Not Your Daddy	Kid Creole and the Coconuts

1983 TOP 40

No	Title	Artist
1	Karma Chameleon	Culture Club
2	Uptown Girl	Billy Joel
3	Every Breath You Take	Police
4	True	Spandau Ballet
5	Only You	Flying Pickets
6	Red Red Wine	UB 40
7	Wherever I Lay My Hat (That's My Home)	Paul Young
8	Down Under	Men At Work
9	Baby Jane	Rod Stewart
10	Give It Up	K.C. and the Sunshine Band
11	Let's Dance	David Bowie
12	You Can't Hurry Love	Phil Collins
13	Total Eclipse Of The Heart	Bonnie Tyler
14	Too Shy	Kajagoogoo
15	Is There Something I Should Know	Duran Duran
16	Save Your Love	Renée and Renato
17	Billie Jean	Michael Jackson
18	Candy Girl	New Edition
19	I.O.U.	Freeez
20	Love Of The Common People	Paul Young
21	All Night Long (All Night)	Lionel Richie
22	Say Say Say	Paul McCartney and Michael Jackson
23	Bad Boys	Wham!
24	They Don't Know	Tracey Ullman
25	My Oh My	Slade
26	Gold	Spandau Ballet
27	Words	F. R. David
28	Church Of The Poison Mind	Culture Club
29	Electric Avenue	Eddy Grant
30	Sweet Dreams (Are Made Of This)	Eurythmics
31	Flashdance...What A Feeling	Irene Cara
32	Keep Feeling Fascination	Human League
33	Tonight I Celebrate My Love	Peabo Bryson and Roberta Flack
34	Modern Love	David Bowie
35	Temptation	Heaven 17
36	A Winter's Tale	David Essex
37	China Girl	David Bowie
38	Wings Of A Dove	Madness
39	The Shakin' Stevens EP	Shakin' Stevens
40	Beat It	Michael Jackson

Michael Jackson

1984   TOP 40

No	Title	Artist
1	Two Tribes	Frankie Goes To Hollywood
2	I Just Called To Say I Love You	Stevie Wonder
3	Hello	Lionel Richie
4	Relax!	Frankie Goes To Hollywood
5	The Reflex	Duran Duran
6	Careless Whisper	George Michael
7	I Feel For You	Chaka Khan
8	99 Red Balloons	Nena
9	Freedom	Wham!
10	Do They Know It's Christmas	Band Aid
11	Wake Me Up Before You Go-Go	Wham!
12	Pipes Of Peace	Paul McCartney
13	I Should Have Known Better	Jim Diamond
14	The Power Of Love	Frankie Goes To Hollywood
15	Only You	Flying Pickets
16	Ghostbusters	Ray Parker Jr.
17	Against All Odds (Take A Look At Me Now)	Phil Collins
18	Hole In My Shoe	neil
19	Last Christmas/Everything She Wants	Wham!
20	Agadoo	Black Lace
21	Joanna/Tonight	Kool And The Gang
22	A Love Worth Waiting For	Shakin' Stevens
23	Let's Hear It For The Boy	Deniece Williams
24	Automatic	Pointer Sisters
25	Radio Ga Ga	Queen
26	Wild Boys	Duran Duran
27	The War Song	Culture Club
28	No More Lonely Nights	Paul McCartney
29	I Won't Let The Sun Go Down On Me	Nik Kershaw
30	You Take Me Up	Thompson Twins
31	Girls Just Want To Have Fun	Cyndi Lauper
32	What Is Love	Howard Jones
33	It's Raining Men	Weather Girls
34	My Oh My	Slade
35	I Want To Break Free	Queen
36	That's Living Alright	Joe Fagin
37	We All Stand Together	Paul McCartney and The Frog Chorus
38	Doctor Doctor	Thompson Twins
39	Street Dance	Break Machine
40	Robert De Niro's Waiting	Bananarama

ionel Richie

1985 TOP 40

No	Title	Artist
1	The Power Of Love	Jennifer Rush
2	19	Paul Hardcastle
3	I Know Him So Well	Elaine Paige and Barbara Dickson
4	Frankie	Sister Sledge
5	Easy Lover	Philip Bailey (duet with Phil Collins)
6	Into The Groove	Madonna
7	Dancing In The Street	David Bowie and Mick Jagger
8	I Want To Know What Love Is	Foreigner
9	I'm Your Man	Wham!
10	Saving All My Love For You	Whitney Houston
11	Do They Know It's Christmas	Band Aid
12	A Good Heart	Feargal Sharkey
13	You Spin Me Round (Like A Record)	Dead Or Alive
14	We Are The World	USA For Africa
15	You'll Never Walk Alone	Crowd
16	I Got You Babe	UB 40 (guest vocals Chrissie Hynde)
17	Move Closer	Phyllis Nelson
18	There Must Be An Angel (Playing With My Heart)	Eurythmics
19	If I Was	Midge Ure
20	Merry Christmas Everyone	Shakin' Stevens
21	Axel F	Harold Faltermeyer
22	Love And Pride	King
23	Take On Me	a-ha
24	A View To A Kill	Duran Duran
25	Holding Out For A Hero	Bonnie Tyler
26	Everybody Wants To Rule The World	Tears For Fears
27	Last Christmas/Everything She Wants	Wham!
28	That Ole Devil Called Love	Alison Moyet
29	Welcome To The Pleasuredome	Frankie Goes To Hollywood
30	Crazy For You	Madonna
31	Kayleigh	Marillion
32	1999/Little Red Corvette	Prince and the Revolution
33	Holiday	Madonna
34	Trapped	Colonel Abrams
35	Solid	Ashford and Simpson
36	See The Day	Dee C. Lee
37	We Don't Need Another Hero (Thunderdome)	Tina Turner
38	Pie Jesu	Sarah Brightman and Paul Miles-Kingston
39	Part-Time Lover	Stevie Wonder
40	I Feel Love (Medley)	Bronski Beat and Marc Almond

Jennifer Rush

1986 TOP 40

No	Title	Artist
1	Don't Leave Me This Way	Communards with Sarah Jane Morris
2	When The Going Gets Tough, The Tough Get Going	Billy Ocean
3	Take My Breath Away (love theme from *Top Gun*)	Berlin
4	Papa Don't Preach	Madonna
5	The Lady In Red	Chris De Burgh
6	Chain Reaction	Diana Ross
7	I Want To Wake Up With You	Boris Gardiner
8	Living Doll	Cliff Richard and the Young Ones featuring Hank B. Marvin
9	A Different Corner	George Michael
10	Every Loser Wins	Nick Berry
11	Spirit In The Sky	Doctor and the Medics
12	The Chicken Song	Spitting Image
13	The Sun Always Shines On T.V.	a-ha
14	The Edge Of Heaven/Where Did Your Heart Go	Wham!
15	The Final Countdown	Europe
16	West End Girls	Pet Shop Boys
17	Rock Me Amadeus	Falco
18	True Blue	Madonna
19	Caravan Of Love	Housemartins
20	Reet Petite	Jackie Wilson
21	Merry Christmas Everyone	Shakin' Stevens
22	On My Own	Patti Labelle and Michael McDonald
23	So Macho/Cruising	Sinitta
24	We Don't Have To...	Jermaine Stewart
25	Rain Or Shine	Five Star
26	You Keep Me Hangin' On	Kim Wilde
27	Holding Back The Years	Simply Red
28	Saving All My Love For You	Whitney Houston
29	I Can't Wait	Nu Shooz
30	In The Army Now	Status Quo
31	Walk Of Life	Dire Straits
32	Borderline	Madonna
33	Manic Monday	Bangles
34	Every Beat Of My Heart	Rod Stewart
35	Sometimes	Erasure
36	Wonderful World	Sam Cooke
37	Starting Together	Su Pollard
38	Absolute Beginners	David Bowie
39	Live To Tell	Madonna
40	Only Love	Nana Mouskouri

David Bowie

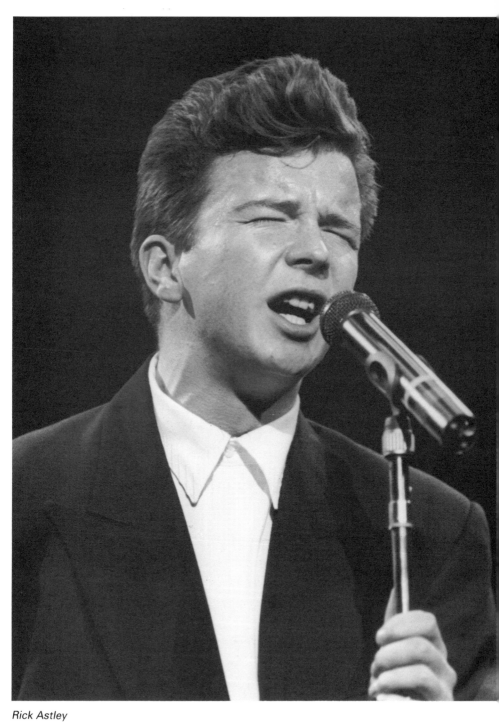

Rick Astley

1987 TOP 40

No	Title	Artist
1	Never Gonna Give You Up	Rick Astley
2	China In Your Hand	T'Pau
3	Nothing's Gonna Stop Us Now	Starship
4	You Win Again	Bee Gees
5	It's A Sin	Pet Shop Boys
6	Reet Petite.	Jackie Wilson
7	Stand By Me	Ben E. King
8	Let It Be	Ferry Aid
9	I Wanna Dance With Somebody (Who Loves Me)	Whitney Houston
10	Pump Up The Volume/Anitina (The First Time I See She Dance).	M/A/R/R/S
11	I Knew You Were Waiting (For Me)	George Michael and Aretha Franklin
12	La Isla Bonita	Madonna
13	Jack Your Body.	Steve 'Silk' Hurley
14	Star Trekkin'	Firm
15	La Bamba	Los Lobos
16	Everything I Own.	Boy George
17	I Just Can't Stop Loving You	Michael Jackson
18	Always On My Mind	Pet Shop Boys
19	Respectable	Mel and Kim
20	Who's That Girl	Madonna
21	Can't Be With You Tonight	Judy Boucher
22	Got My Mind Set On You	George Harrison
23	Under The Boardwalk	Bruce Willis
24	Full Metal Jacket (I Wanna Be Your Drill Instructor).	Abigail Mead and Nigel Goulding
25	What Have I Done To Deserve This	Pet Shop Boys and Dusty Springfield
26	Heartache	Pepsi and Shirlie
27	When I Fall In Love/My Arms Keep Missing You.	Rick Astley
28	When A Man Loves A Woman	Percy Sledge
29	Faith	George Michael
30	Caravan Of Love.	Housemartins
31	Hold Me Now	Johnny Logan
32	Wipeout	Fat Boys and Beach Boys
33	A Boy From Nowhere	Tom Jones
34	Call Me	Spagna
35	Crockett's Theme	Jan Hammer
36	Fairytale Of New York	Pogues and Kirsty MacColl
37	Is This Love	Alison Moyet
38	Whenever You Need Somebody.	Rick Astley
39	Down To Earth	Curiosity Killed The Cat
40	I Get The Sweetest Feeling	Jackie Wilson

THE
ARTISTS

An alphabetical listing, by artist name,
of the Top 1000 hits.

Rank	Title	Label & No.

A

ABBA
41 Dancing Queen .... Epic EPC 4499
62 Knowing Me Knowing You Epic EPC 4955
97 Fernando .... Epic EPC 4036
173 The Name Of The Game ... Epic EPC 5750
202 Take A Chance On Me ..... Epic EPC 5950
273 Super Trouper .... Epic EPC 9089
381 Waterloo .... Epic EPC 2240
391 Mamma Mia .... Epic EPC 3790
426 The Winner Takes It All.... Epic EPC 8835
595 I Have A Dream .... Epic EPC 8088
742 Chiquitita .... Epic EPC 7030

FATHER ABRAHAM AND THE SMURFS
570 The Smurf Song .... Decca F 13759

ADAM AND THE ANTS
91 Stand And Deliver .... CBS A 1065
144 Prince Charming .... CBS A 1408
335 Goody Two Shoes .... CBS A 2367
766 Antmusic .... CBS 9352
992 Kings Of The Wild Frontier ... CBS 8877
Goody Two Shoes *credited to Adam Ant*

A-HA
374 The Sun Always Shines On T.V. ......
.... Warner Brothers W 8846
633 Take On Me ...... Warner Brothers W 9006

ALICE COOPER
263 School's Out ...... Warner Brothers K 16188

ALLISONS
568 Are You Sure .... Fontana H 294

ALTERED IMAGES
666 Happy Birthday .... Epic EPC A 1522

ALTHIA AND DONNA
505 Up Town Top Ranking .. Lightning LIG 506

AMEN CORNER
384 (If Paradise Is) Half As Nice ....
.... Immediate IM 073

LAURIE ANDERSON
972 O Superman ...... Warner Brothers K 17870

ANEKA
542 Japanese Boy .... Hansa HANSA 5

ANIMALS
556 House Of The Rising Sun Columbia DB 7301
924 We've Gotta Get Out Of This Place ....
.... Columbia DB 7639

PAUL ANKA
3 Diana .... Columbia DB 3980

ARCHIES
9 Sugar Sugar .... RCA 1872

LOUIS ARMSTRONG
131 What A Wonderful World/Cabaret ...
.... HMV POP 1615

RICK ASTLEY
72 Never Gonna Give You Up . RCA PB 41447

Rank	Title	Label & No.
786	When I Fall In Love/My Arms Keep Missing You .... RCA PB 41683
790	Together Forever .... RCA PB 41817

WINIFRED ATWELL
185 Poor People Of Paris ...... Decca F 10681

WINIFRED ATWELL, DAVE KING, JOAN REGAN, LITA ROZA, DICKIE VALENTINE AND DAVID WHITFIELD
926 All Star Hit Parade .... Decca F 10752

CHARLES AZNAVOUR
148 She .... Barclay BAR 26

B

BACCARA
478 Yes Sir I Can Boogie .... RCA PB 5526

BACHELORS
525 Diane .... Decca F 11799
801 I Believe .... Decca F 11857

BACHMAN-TURNER OVERDRIVE
736 You Ain't Seen Nothin' Yet ....
.... Mercury 6167 025

PHILIP BAILEY
138 Easy Lover .... CBS A 4915
Hit has credit 'duet with Phil Collins'.
See also Phil Collins

LONG JOHN BALDRY
411 Let The Heartaches Begin . Pye 7N 17385

KENNY BALL AND HIS JAZZMEN
953 Midnight In Moscow .. Pye Jazz 7NJ 2049

BAND AID
67 Do They Know It's Christmas ....
.... Mercury FEED 1

BANGLES
942 Manic Monday .... CBS A 6796

J.J. BARRIE
497 No Charge .... Power Exchange PX 209

TONI BASIL
749 Mickey .... Radialchoice TIC 4

SHIRLEY BASSEY
103 As I Love You .... Phillips PB 845
479 Reach For The Stars/Climb Ev'ry Mountain .... Columbia DB 4685
576 As Long As He Needs Me ....
.... Columbia DB 4490

BAY CITY ROLLERS
39 Bye Bye Baby .... Bell 1409
282 Give A Little Love .... Bell 1425
994 Shang-A-Lang .... Bell 1355

BEACH BOYS
373 Good Vibrations .... Capitol CL 15475
538 Do It Again .... Capitol CL 15554
695 God Only Knows .... Capitol CL 15459
957 Sloop John B. .... Capitol CL 15441
See also Fat Boys and The Beach Boys

Rank	Title	Label & No.

BEATLES
- 15 From Me To You . . . . Parlophone R 5015
- 21 Hello Goodbye . . . . Parlophone R 5655
- 22 She Loves You . . . . Parlophone R 5055
- 38 Get Back . . . . Apple R 5777
- 61 Day Tripper/We Can Work It Out . . . . . Parlophone R 5389
- 75 I Want To Hold Your Hand . . . . Parlophone R 5084
- 82 I Feel Fine . . . . Parlophone R 5200
- 168 Yellow Submarine/Eleanor Rigby . . . . Parlophone R 5493
- 197 All You Need Is Love . . . Parlophone R 5620
- 211 A Hard Day's Night . . . . Parlophone R 5160
- 225 Help . . . . Parlophone R 5305
- 264 Ticket To Ride . . . . Parlophone R 5265
- 279 Can't Buy Me Love . . . . . Parlophone R 5114
- 302 Ballad Of John And Yoko . . . Apple R 5786
- 327 Hey Jude . . . . Apple R 5722
- 383 Paperback Writer . . . . . . Parlophone R 5452
- 449 Lady Madonna . . . . Parlophone R 5675
- 601 Please Please Me . . . . . . Parlophone R 4983
- 623 Magical Mystery Tour (Double EP) . . . . Parlophone SMMT/MMT 1
- 659 Penny Lane/Strawberry Fields Forever . . . . Parlophone R 5570
- 936 Let It Be . . . . Apple R 5833
  Get Back *is with Billy Preston – see also Billy Preston & Syreeta*

BEE GEES
- 114 Massachusetts . . . . Polydor 56 192
- 170 You Win Again . . . . Warner Brothers W 8351
- 324 Night Fever . . . . RSO 002
- 410 Tragedy . . . . RSO 27
- 488 I've Gotta Get A Message To You . . . . Polydor 56 263
- 866 Don't Forget To Remember Polydor 56 343

HARRY BELAFONTE
- 19 Mary's Boy Child . . . . RCA 1022
- 600 Banana Boat Song . . . . HMV POP 308

LA BELLE EPOQUE
- 626 Black Is Black . . . . Harvest HAR 5133

BERLIN
- 146 Take My Breath Away (Love theme from *Top Gun*) . . . . CBS A 7320

CHUCK BERRY
- 101 My Ding-A-Ling . . . . Chess 6145 019

NICK BERRY
- 283 Every Loser Wins . . . . BBC RESL 204

MR. ACKER BILK
- 661 Stranger On The Shore . Columbia DB 4750

JANE BIRKIN AND SERGE GAINSBOURG
- 485 Je T'Aime . . . Moi Non Plus . . . . Fontana TF 1042

CILLA BLACK
- 167 You're My World . . . . . . Parlophone R 5133
- 254 Anyone Who Had A Heart . . . . Parlophone R 5101

Rank	Title	Label & No.

BLACK LACE
- 687 Agadoo . . . . Flair FLA 107

BLONDIE
- 149 Heart Of Glass . . . . Chrysalis CHS 2275
- 281 Sunday Girl . . . . Chrysalis CHS 2320
- 375 The Tide Is High . . . . Chrysalis CHS 2465
- 414 Atomic . . . . Chrysalis CHS 2410
- 545 Call Me . . . . Chrysalis CHS 2414
- 631 Denis . . . . Chrysalis CHS 2204
- 935 Dreaming . . . . Chrysalis CHS 2350

BARRY BLUE
- 771 (Dancing) On A Saturday Night Bell 1295

BOMB THE BASS
- 744 Beat Dis . . . . . Mister-On/Rhythm King DOOD 1

BONEY M
- 50 Rivers Of Babylon/Brown Girl In The Ring . . . . Atlantic/Hansa K 11120
- 153 Mary's Boy Child/Oh My Lord . . . . Atlantic/Hansa K 11221
- 723 Rasputin . . . . Atlantic/Hansa K 11192
- 840 Ma Baker . . . . Atlantic K 10965

BOOMTOWN RATS
- 123 I Don't Like Mondays . . . . . Ensign ENY 30
- 348 Rat Trap . . . . Ensign ENY 16

BOY GEORGE
- 433 Everything I Own . . . . Virgin BOY 100

PAT BOONE
- 51 I'll Be Home . . . . London HLD 8253
- 567 Love Letters In The Sand London HLD 8445
- 574 Don't Forbid Me . . . . London HLD 8370
- 583 Speedy Gonzales . . . . London HLD 9573
- 890 A Wonderful Time Up There . . . . London HLD 8574

KEN BOOTHE
- 260 Everything I Own . . . . Trojan TR 7920

JUDY BOUCHER
- 588 Can't Be With You Tonight Orbitone OR 721

DAVID BOWIE
- 293 Let's Dance . . . . EMI America EA 152
- 365 Space Oddity . . . . Phillips BF 1801
- 397 Ashes to Ashes . . . . RCA BOW 6
- 850 The Jean Genie . . . . RCA 2302
- 938 Modern Love . . . . EMI America EA 158
- 969 China Girl . . . . EMI America EA 157
- 970 Absolute Beginners . . . . Virgin VS 838
  See also David Bowie and Mick Jagger, Queen and David Bowie

DAVID BOWIE AND MICK JAGGER
- 171 Dancing In The Street . EMI America EA 204
  See also David Bowie, Queen and David Bowie

LOS BRAVOS
- 901 Black Is Black . . . . Decca F 22419

TERESA BREWER
- 978 A Tear Fell . . . . Vogue/Coral Q 72146

BRIAN AND MICHAEL
- 241 Matshstalk Men and Matchstalk Cats and Dogs . . . . Pye 7N 46035

Rank	Title	Label & No.

BRIGHOUSE AND RASTRICK BRASS BAND
571 The Floral Dance ..... Transatlantic BIG 548
BROS
966 When Will I Be Famous .... CBS ATOM 2
BROTHERHOOD OF MAN
32 Save Your Kisses For Me .. Pye 7N 45569
458 Angelo .... Pye 7N 45699
489 Figaro.................. Pye 7N 46037
CRAZY WORLD OF ARTHUR BROWN
502 Fire .... Track 604 022
JOE BROWN AND THE BRUVVERS
677 A Picture Of You ...... Piccadilly 7N 35047
PEABO BRYSON AND ROBERTA FLACK
931 Tonight I Celebrate My Love Capitol CL 302
BUCKS FIZZ
274 Making Your Mind Up.......... RCA 56
364 The Land Of Make Believe ..... RCA 163
520 My Camera Never Lies .... RCA 202
BUGGLES
517 Video Killed The Radio Star ....
.... Island WIP 6524
B. BUMBLE AND THE STINGERS
475 Nut Rocker .... Top Rank JAR 611
LOU BUSCH
582 Zambesi .... Capitol CL 14504
KATE BUSH
169 Wuthering Heights .... EMI 2719
MAX BYGRAVES
911 Meet Me On The Corner ... HMV POP 116
BYRDS
398 Mr. Tambourine Man ...... CBS 201765

C

CANNED HEAT
827 Let's Work Together ... Liberty LBF 15302
CAPTAIN SENSIBLE
448 Happy Talk .... A & M CAP 1
IRENE CARA
208 Fame .... RSO 90
892 Flashdance...What A Feeling ......
.... Casablanca CAN 1016
BELINDA CARLISLE
350 Heaven Is A Place On Earth Virgin VS 1036
CARPENTERS
763 Yesterday Once More ... A & M AMS 7073
881 Please Mr. Postman .... A & M AMS 7141
VIKKI CARR
914 It Must Be Him (Seul Sur Son Etoile) ..
.... Liberty LIB 55917
CLARENCE CARTER
629 Patches .... Atlantic 2091 030
DAVID CASSIDY
266 Daydreamer/The Puppy Song Bell 1334
400 How Can I Be Sure .... Bell 1258
858 Could It Be Forever/Cherish .. Bell 1224
CASUALS
804 Jesamine................ Decca F 22784

Rank	Title	Label & No.

BRUCE CHANNEL
894 Hey! Baby .... Mercury AMT 1171
CHARLENE
549 I've Never Been To Me . Motown TMG 1260
RAY CHARLES
338 I Can't Stop Loving You ... HMV POP 1034
TINA CHARLES
244 I Love To Love (But My Baby Loves To Dance) .... CBS 3937
CHAS AND DAVE
993 Ain't No Pleasing You .... Rockney KOR 14
CHUBBY CHECKER
679 Let's Twist Again ...... Columbia DB 4691
CHICAGO
207 If You Leave Me Now .... CBS 4603
CHICORY TIP
255 Son Of My Father .... CBS 7737
CHRISTIE
476 Yellow River .... CBS 4911
LOU CHRISTIE
829 I'm Gonna Make You Mine Buddah 201 057
TONY CHRISTIE
751 I Did What I Did For Maria . MCA MK 5064
PETULA CLARK
437 This Is My Song .... Pye 7N 17258
459 Sailor .... Pye 7N 15324
643 Downtown .... Pye 7N 15722
DAVE CLARK FIVE
329 Glad All Over .... Columbia DB 7154
654 Bits And Pieces .... Columbia DB 7210
708 Everybody Knows ..... Columbia DB 8286
CLOUT
693 Substitute .... Carrere EMI 2788
EDDIE COCHRAN
339 Three Steps To Heaven .. London HLG 9115
JOE COCKER
519 With A Little Help From My Friends...
.... Regal-Zonophone RZ 3013
NAT 'KING' COLE
799 When I Fall In Love ..... Capitol CL 14709
DAVE AND ANSIL COLLINS
395 Double Barrel .... Technique TE 901
PHIL COLLINS
353 You Can't Hurry Love ...... Virgin VS 531
628 Against All Odds (Take A Look At Me Now) .... Virgin VS 674
897 In The Air Tonight .... Virgin VSK 102
See also Philip Bailey
COMMODORES with SARAH JANE MORRIS
79 Three Times A Lady .... Motown TMG 1113
COMMUNARDS
134 Don't Leave Me This Way . London LON 103
PERRY COMO
6 Magic Moments .... RCA 1036
BILLY CONNOLLY
550 D.I.V.O.R.C.E. .... Polydor 2058 652
RUSS CONWAY
124 Side Saddle .... Columbia DB 4256

Rank	Title	Label & No.
361	Roulette	Columbia DB 4298

SAM COOKE

962	Wonderful World	HMV POP 754

ELVIS COSTELLO AND THE ATTRACTIONS

621	Oliver's Army	Radar ADA 31

JULIE COVINGTON

455	Don't Cry For Me Argentina . . .	MCA 260

FLOYD CRAMER

565	On The Rebound	RCA 1231

RANDY CRAWFORD

780	One Day I'll Fly Away . . . .
	. . . .	Warner Brothers K 17680

CREEDENCE CLEARWATER REVIVAL

217	Bad Moon Rising	Liberty LBF 15230

CRICKETS

243	That'll Be The Day	Vogue Coral Q 72279

CROWD

445	You'll Never Walk Alone . .	Spartan BRAD 1

CRYSTALS

717	Then He Kissed Me	London HLU 9773

CULTURE CLUB

43	Karma Chameleon	Virgin VS 612
252	Do You Really Want To Hurt Me . . . . . .
	. . . .	Virgin VS 518
794	Church Of The Poison Mind .	Virgin VS 571
883	The War Song	Virgin VS 694

D

TERRY DACTYL AND THE DINOSAURS

774	Seaside Shuffle	UK 5

JIM DALE

797	Be My Girl	Parlophone R 4343

VIC DAMONE

341	On The Street Where You Live . . . .
	. . . .	Phillips PB 819

DANA

351	All Kinds Of Everything	Rex R 11054

TERENCE TRENT D'ARBY

945	Sign Your Name	CBS TRENT 4

BOBBY DARIN

93	Dream Lover	London HLE 8867
322	Mack The Knife	London HLE 8939
839	Things	London HLK 9575
965	Lazy River	London HLK 9303

DARTS

816	Boy From New York City .	Magnet MAG 116
836	Come Back My Love	Magnet MAG 110
838	It's Raining	Magnet MAG 126

F. R. DAVID

772	Words	Carrere CAR 248

WINDSOR DAVIES AND DON ESTELLE

200	Whispering Grass	EMI 2290

SPENCER DAVIS GROUP

417	Somebody Help Me	Fontana TF 679
469	Keep On Running	Fontana TF 632

Rank	Title	Label & No.
918	Gimme Some Loving	Fontana TF 762

DAWN

58	Knock Three Times	Bell 1146
127	Tie A Yellow Ribbon Round The Old
	Oak Tree	Bell 1287

DORIS DAY

23	Whatever Will Be Will Be . .	Phillips PB 586

CHRIS DE BURGH

218	The Lady In Red	A & M AM 331

STEPHANIE DE SYKES WITH RAIN

879	Born With A Smile On My Face . . . . . .
	. . . .	Bradley's BRAD 7409

DEAD OR ALIVE

429	You Spin Me Round (Like A Record) . .
	. . . .	Epic A 4861

JIMMY DEAN

810	Big Bad John	Phillips PB 1187

DAVE DEE, DOZY, BEAKY, MICK AND TICH

496	Legend of Xanadu	Fontana TF 903
756	Bend It	Fontana TF 746

DEEP PURPLE

697	Black Night	Harvest HAR 5020

DESMOND DEKKER AND THE ACES

529	Israelites	Pyramid PYR 6058
726	You Can Get It If You Really Want . . . . .
	. . . .	Trojan TR 7777
	You Can Get It If You Really Want
	credited simply to Desmond Dekker

JOHN DENVER

491	Annie's Song	RCA APBO 0295

DETROIT SPINNERS

442	Working My Way Back To You/Forgive
	Me Girl	Atlantic K 11432

DEXY'S MIDNIGHT RUNNERS

110	Come On Eileen	Mercury DEXYS 9
376	Geno	Late Night Feelings R 6033
	Dexys Midnight Runners has no apostrophe on Come On Eileen

JIM DIAMOND

504	I Should Have Known Better . . . .
	. . . .	A & M AM 220

DIRE STRAITS

920	Walk Of Life	Vertigo DSTR 12
946	Private Investigations . . . .
	. . . .	Vertigo DSTR 1

DOCTOR AND THE MEDICS

309	Spirit In The Sky	IRS IRM 113

DR. HOOK

209	When You're In Love With A Beautiful
	Woman	Capitol CL 16039
572	A Little Bit More	Capitol CL 15871
846	Sylvia's Mother	CBS 7929
	Sylvia's Mother *credited to Dr. Hook and the Medicine Show*

KEN DODD

54	Tears	Columbia DB 7659

JOE DOLCE MUSIC THEATRE

306	Shaddup You Face	Epic EPC 9518

116

Rank	Title	Label & No.

FIRM
418 Star Trekkin' . . . . Bark TREK 1
FIVE STAR
724 Rain Or Shine . . . . Tent PB 40901
FLEETWOOD MAC
453 Albatross . . . . Blue Horizon 57 3145
711 Oh Well . . . . Reprise RS 27000
814 Man Of The World . . . . . . Immediate IM 080
FLOATERS
537 Float On . . . . ABC 4187
FLYING PICKETS
92 Only You . . . . 10 TEN 14
WAYNE FONTANA AND THE MINDBENDERS
955 Game Of Love . . . . Fontana TF 535
See also Mindbenders
EMILE FORD AND THE CHECKMATES
25 What Do You Want To Make Those Eyes At Me For . . . . Pye 7N 15225
TENNESSEE ERNIE FORD
117 Sixteen Tons . . . .-. Capitol CL 14500
FOREIGNER
308 I Want To Know What Love Is . . . . Atlantic A 9596
FORTUNES
828 You've Got Your Troubles . . Decca F 12173
FOUNDATIONS
363 Baby Now That I've Found You . . . . Pye 7N 17366
681 Build Me Up Buttercup . . . . Pye 7N 17638
FOUR ACES
673 Love Is A Many Splendoured Thing . . . . Brunswick 05480
FOUR PENNIES
492 Juliet . . . . Phillips BF 1322
FOUR PREPS
714 Big Man . . . . Capitol CL 14873
FOUR SEASONS
356 December '63 (Oh What A Night) . . . . Warner Brothers K 16688
775 Rag Doll . . . . Phillips BF 1347
FOUR TOPS
251 Reach Out I'll Be There . . . . Tamla Motown TMG 579
CONNIE FRANCIS
27 Who's Sorry Now . . . . MGM 975
30 Carolina Moon/Stupid Cupid . MGM 985
835 Mama/Robot Man . . . . MGM 1076
FRANKIE GOES TO HOLLYWOOD
4 Two Tribes . . . . ZTT ZTAS 3
48 Relax! . . . . ZTT ZTAS 1
560 The Power Of Love . . . . ZTT ZTAS 5
791 Welcome To The Pleasuredome . . . . ZTT ZTAS 7
ARETHA FRANKLIN AND GEORGE MICHAEL
378 I Knew You Were Waiting (For Me) . . . . Epic DUET 2
See also George Michael

Rank	Title	Label & No.

FREDDIE AND THE DREAMERS
737 I'm Telling You Now . . . Columbia DB 7068
FREE
575 All Right Now . . . . Island WIP 6082
FREEEZ
610 I.O.U. . . . . Beggars Banquet BEG 96
BILLY FURY
980 Jealousy . . . . Decca F 11384

G

BORIS GARDINER
226 I Want To Wake Up With You . . . . Revue REV 733
ART GARFUNKEL
44 Bright Eyes . . . . CBS 6947
346 I Only Have Eyes For You . . . . . CBS 3575
See also Simon and Garfunkel
MARVIN GAYE
210 I Heard It Through The Grapevine . . . . Tamla Motown TMG 686
GLORIA GAYNOR
164 I Will Survive . . . . Polydor 2095 017
981 Never Can Say Goodbye . . MGM 2006 463
BOBBIE GENTRY
466 I'll Never Fall In Love Again . . . . Capitol CL 15606
GERRY AND THE PACEMAKERS
115 You'll Never Walk Alone Columbia DB 7126
119 I Like It . . . . Columbia DB 7041
199 How Do You Do It . . . . . . Columbia DB 4987
767 I'm The One . . . . Columbia DB 7189
ROBIN GIBB
684 Saved By The Bell . . . . Polydor 56337
GARY GLITTER
96 I Love You Love Me Love . . . . . Bell 1337
135 I'm The Leader Of The Gang (I Am) . . . . Bell 1321
547 Always Yours . . . . Bell 1359
619 Hello Hello I'm Back Again . . . . Bell 1299
634 Rock and Roll (Parts 1 and 2) . . Bell 1216
698 Do You Wanna Touch Me (Oh Yeah) . . . . Bell 1280
947 Oh Yes! You're Beautiful . . . . . . Bell 1391
GLITTER BAND
997 Goodbye My Love . . . . Bell 1395
BOBBY GOLDSBORO
676 Honey . . . . United Artists UP 2215
GOOMBAY DANCE BAND
285 Seven Tears . . . . Epic EPC A 1242
EDDY GRANT
284 I Don't Wanna Dance . . . . Ice ICE 56
864 Electric Avenue . . . . Ice ICE 57
NORMAN GREENBAUM
332 Spirit In The Sky . . . . Reprise RS 20885
GUYS AND DOLLS
721 There's A Whole Lot Of Loving . . . . Magnet MAG 20

Rank	Title	Label & No.

H

BILL HALEY AND HIS COMETS
49 Rock Around The Clock . Brunswick 05317
RUSS HAMILTON
843 We Will Make Love . . . . Oriole CB 1359
JAN HAMMER
979 Crockett's Theme . . . . MCA MCA 1193
PAUL HARDCASTLE
85 19 . . . . Chrysalis CHS 2860
STEVE HARLEY AND COCKNEY REBEL
416 Make Me Smile (Come Up And See Me)
. . . . EMI 2263
JET HARRIS AND TONY MEEHAN
307 Diamond . . . . Decca F 11563
842 Scarlett O'Hara . . . . Decca F 11644
ROLF HARRIS
29 Two Little Boys . . . . Columbia DB 8630
GEORGE HARRISON
74 My Sweet Lord . . . . Apple R 5884
594 Got My Mind Set On You . . . .
. . . . Dark Horse W 8178
EDWIN HAWKINS SINGERS
745 Oh Happy Day . . . . Buddah 201 048
BILL HAYES
636 Ballad Of Davy Crockett . London HLA 8220
HEATWAVE
852 Boogie Nights . . . . GTO GT 77
HEAVEN 17
941 Temptation . . . . B.E.F. VS 570
JIMI HENDRIX EXPERIENCE
514 Voodoo Chile . . . . Track 2095 001
HERMAN'S HERMITS
349 I'm Into Something Good Columbia DB 7338
777 My Sentimental Friend . Columbia DB 8563
HIGHWAYMEN
534 Michael . . . . HMV POP 910
BENNY HILL
104 Ernie (The Fastest Milkman In The
West) . . . . Columbia DB 8833
VINCE HILL
915 Edelweiss . . . . Columbia DB 8127
RONNIE HILTON
45 No Other Love . . . . HMV POP 198
MICHAEL HOLLIDAY
320 The Story Of My Life . . . Columbia DB 4058
559 Starry Eyed . . . . Columbia DB 4378
HOLLIES
269 I'm Alive . . . . Parlophone R 5287
641 I Can't Let Go . . . . Parlophone R 5409
785 Stop Stop Stop . . . . Parlophone R 5508
815 The Air That I Breathe . . . Polydor 2058 435
951 Just One Look . . . . Parlophone R 5104
BUDDY HOLLY
180 It Doesn't Matter Anymore Coral Q 72360
HONEYCOMBS
340 Have I The Right . . . . Pye 7N 15664

Rank	Title	Label & No.

MARY HOPKIN
33 Those Were The Days . . . . Apple 2
635 Goodbye . . . . Apple 10
984 Knock Knock Who's There . . . . . Apple 26
HOT CHOCOLATE
247 So You Win Again . . . . RAK 259
616 You Sexy Thing . . . . RAK 221
650 No Doubt About It . . . . RAK 310
HOTLEGS
702 Neanderthal Man . . . . . . Fontana 6007 019
HOUSEMARTINS
461 Caravan Of Love . . . . Go! Discs GOD 16
WHITNEY HOUSTON
326 Saving All My Love For You . . . .
. . . . Arista ARIST 640
333 I Wanna Dance With Somebody (Who
Loves Me) . . . . Arista RIS 1
HUMAN LEAGUE
80 Don't You Want Me . . . . Virgin VS 466
671 Mirror Man . . . . Virgin VS 522
930 (Keep Feeling) Fascination . Virgin VS 569
ENGELBERT HUMPERDINCK
31 Release Me . . . . Decca F 12541
64 The Last Waltz . . . . Decca F 12655
590 There Goes My Everything . Decca F 12610
617 A Man Without Love . . . . . . Decca F 12770
TAB HUNTER
10 Young Love . . . . London HLD 8380
STEVE 'SILK' HURLEY
415 Jack Your Body . . . . DJ International LON 117

I

IAN AND THE BLOCKHEADS
464 Hit Me With Your Rhythm Stick . . . . . .
. . . . Stiff BUY 38
FRANK IFIELD
12 I Remember You . . . . . . Columbia DB 4856
65 Lovesick Blues . . . . Columbia DB 4913
280 Wayward Wind . . . . Columbia DB 4960
323 Confessin' . . . . Columbia DB 7062
JULIO IGLESIAS
532 Begin The Beguine (Volver A Empezar)
. . . . CBS A 1612
IMAGINATION
937 Just An Illusion . . . . R & B RBS 208

J

TERRY JACKS
162 Seasons In The Sun . . . . Bell 1344
MICHAEL JACKSON
352 One Day In Your Life . . . . Motown TMG 976
495 Billie Jean . . . . Epic EPC A 3084
447 I Just Can't Stop Loving You . . . .
. . . . Epic 650202 7

*See also Paul
McCartney & Michael
Jackson, Jacksons,
Jackson Five*

Rank	Title	Label & No.

JACKSON FIVE
974   I Want You Back .... Tamla Motown TMG 724
     See also Jacksons, Michael Jackson,
     Paul McCartney & Michael Jackson

JACKSONS
501   Show You The Way To Go . Epic EPC 5266
     See also Jackson Five, Michael
     Jackson, Paul McCartney &
     Michael Jackson

JAM
313   Going Underground/Dreams Of
     Children . . . . Polydor POSP 113
316   Town Called Malice/Precious . . . .
     . . . . Polydor POSP 400
436   Beat Surrender . . . . Polydor POSP 540
499   Start . . . . Polydor 2059 266
796   The Bitterest Pill (I Ever Had To
     Swallow) . . . . Polydor POSP 505

**TOMMY JAMES AND THE
SHONDELLS**
222   Mony Mony . . . . Major Minor MM 567

BILLY JOEL
86   Uptown Girl . . . . CBS A 3775

ELTON JOHN AND KIKI DEE
36   Don't Go Breaking My Heart . . . .
     . . . . Rocket ROKN 512

HOWARD JONES
949   What Is Love . . . . WEA HOW 2

JIMMY JONES
201   Good Timin' . . . . MGM 1078

TOM JONES
14   Green Green Grass Of Home . . . .
     . . . . Decca F 22511
460   It's Not Unusual . . . . Decca F 12062
584   I'll Never Fall In Love Again . . . .
     . . . . Decca F 12639
618   Delilah . . . . Decca F 12747
871   I'm Coming Home . . . . Decca F 12693
906   A Boy From Nowhere . . . . Epic OLE 1
991   Till . . . . Decca F 13236

K

KAJAGOOGOO
405   Too Shy . . . . EMI 5359

KALIN TWINS
63   When . . . . Brunswick 05751

EDEN KANE
483   Well I Ask You . . . . Decca F 11353

JANET KAY
705   Silly Games . . . . Scope SC 2

K.C. AND THE SUNSHINE BAND
276   Give It Up . . . . Epic EPC A 3017

JERRY KELLER
474   Here Comes Summer . . . London HLR 8890

NIK KERSHAW
907   I Won't Let The Sun Go Down On Me . .
     . . . . MCA 816

CHAKA KHAN
228   I Feel For You . . . . . Warner Brothers W 9209

JOHNNY KIDD AND THE PIRATES
524   Shakin' All Over . . . . HMV POP 753

KING
625   Love And Pride . . . . CBS A 4988

BEN E. KING
296   Stand By Me . . . . London HLK 9358

KINKS
404   Sunny Afternoon . . . . Pye 7N 17125
425   You Really Got Me . . . . . . Pye 7N 15673
515   Tired Of Waiting For You . . Pye 7N 15759
701   Waterloo Sunset . . . . Pye 7N 17321
793   All Day And All Of The Night Pye 7N 15714
832   Lola . . . . Pye 7N 17961

FERN KINNEY
471   Together We Are Beautiful   WEA K 79111

KOOL AND THE GANG
729   Joanna/Tonight . . . . De-Lite DE 16

KRAFTWERK
539   Computer Love/The Model . . . EMI 5207

**BILLY J. KRAMER AND THE
DAKOTAS**
300   Bad To Me . . . . Parlophone R 5049
344   Little Children . . . . Parlophone R 5105
692   Do You Want To Know A Secret . . . . . .
     . . . . Parlophone R 5023

L

**PATTI LABELLE AND MICHAEL
  McDONALD**
656   On My Own . . . . MCA MCA 1045

FRANKIE LAINE
94   A Woman In Love . . . . Phillips PB 617

GREG LAKE
831   I Believe In Father Christmas . . . .
     . . . . Manticore K 13511
     See also Emerson, Lake and Palmer

CYNDI LAUPER
943   Girls Just Wanna Have Fun Portrait A 3943

**LAUREL AND HARDY
  WITH THE AVALON BOYS**
614   The Trail Of The Lonesome Pine . . . . . .
     . . . . United Artists UP 36026

VICKY LEANDROS
895   Come What May . . . . Phillips 6000 049

LEAPY LEE
973   Little Arrows . . . . MCA MU 1028

JOHN LENNON
174   Imagine . . . . Apple R 6009
388   Woman . . . . Geffen K 79195
513   (Just Like) Starting Over . . Geffen K 79186
646   Give Peace A Chance . . . . Apple 13
888   Happy Xmas (War Is Over) . . Apple R 5970

JERRY LEE LEWIS
451   Great Balls Of Fire . . . . . . London HLS 8529

JOHN LEYTON
98   Johnny Remember Me . . Top Rank JAR 577
792   Wild Wind . . . . Top Rank JAR 585

LIEUTENANT PIGEON
133   Mouldy Old Dough . . . . Decca F 13278

Rank	Title	Label & No.
LIPPS INC.		
685	Funky Town	Casablanca CAN 194
LIQUID GOLD		
716	Dance Yourself Dizzy	Polo 1
LITTLE EVA		
630	The Loco-Motion	London HL 9581
LITTLE RICHARD		
870	Baby Face	London HLU 8770
LOS LOBOS		
430	La Bamba	Slash/FF LASH 13
JOHNNY LOGAN		
419	What's Another Year	Epic EPC 8572
856	Hold Me Now	Epic LOG 1
LOVE AFFAIR		
345	Everlasting Love	CBS 3125
LOVIN' SPOONFUL		
755	Daydream	Pye International 7N 25361
LULU		
987	Boom Bang-A-Bang	Columbia DB 8550

M

Rank	Title	Label & No.
M		
683	Pop Muzik	MCA 413
C. W. McCALL		
859	Convoy	MGM 2006 560
PAUL McCARTNEY		
2	Mull Of Kintyre/Girls' School	
		Capitol R 6018
434	Pipes Of Peace	Parlophone R 6064
662	Let 'Em In	Parlophone R 6015
710	Another Day	Apple R 5889
872	Silly Love Songs	Parlophone R 6014
885	Coming Up	Parlophone R 6035
903	No More Lonely Nights	Parlophone R 6080
	Mull Of Kintyre, Let 'Em In and Silly Love Songs credited to Wings	
PAUL McCARTNEY AND MICHAEL JACKSON		
706	Say Say Say	Parlophone R 6062
	See also Paul McCartney, Paul McCartney with Stevie Wonder, Michael Jackson, Jacksons, Jackson Five	
PAUL McCARTNEY WITH STEVIE WONDER		
267	Ebony And Ivory	Parlophone R 6054
	See also Paul McCartney, Stevie Wonder, Paul McCartney and Michael Jackson	
GEORGE McCRAE		
248	Rock Your Baby	Jayboy BOY 85
McGUINNESS FLINT		
597	When I'm Dead And Gone	
		Capitol CL 15662
SCOTT McKENZIE		
125	San Francisco (Be Sure To Wear Flowers In Your Hair)	CBS 2816

Rank	Title	Label & No.
DON McLEAN		
270	Crying	EMI 5051
372	Vincent	United Artists UP 35359
607	American Pie	United Artists UP 35325
RALPH McTELL		
765	Streets Of London	Reprise K 14380
M/A/R/R/S		
354	Pump Up The Volume/Anitina (The First Time I See She Dance)	4AD AD 707
MADNESS		
432	House Of Fun	Stiff BUY 146
996	Wings Of A Dove	Stiff BUY 181
MADONNA		
140	Into The Groove	Sire W 8934
215	Papa Don't Preach	Sire W 8636
389	La Isla Bonita	Sire W 8378
498	True Blue	Sire W 8550
507	Who's That Girl	Sire W 8341
820	Crazy For You	Geffen A 6323
929	Borderline	Sire W 9260
956	Holiday	Sire W 9405
995	Live To Tell	Sire W 8717
MAMAS AND THE PAPAS		
823	Dedicated To The One I Love	RCA 1576
MANFRED MANN		
288	Pretty Flamingo	HMV POP 1523
355	Mighty Quinn	Fontana TF 897
366	Do Wah Diddy Diddy	HMV POP 1320
874	If You Gotta Go Go Now	HMV POP 1466
954	Semi-Detached Suburban Mr. James	Fontana TF 757
MANHATTAN TRANSFER		
303	Chanson D'Amour	Atlantic K 10886
MARCELS		
407	Blue Moon	Pye International 7N 25073
KELLY MARIE		
444	Feels Like I'm In Love	Calibre PLUS 1
MARILLION		
905	Kayleigh	EMI MARIL 3
MARINO MARINI		
651	Come Prima	Durium DC 16632
MARMALADE		
310	Ob-La-Di Ob-La-Da	CBS 3892
LENA MARTELL		
291	One Day At A Time	Pye 7N 46021
DEAN MARTIN		
159	Memories Are Made Of This	Capitol CL 14523
606	Volare	Capitol CL 14910
800	Return To Me	Capitol CL 14844
977	Gentle On My Mind	Reprise RS 23343
TONY MARTIN		
806	Walk Hand In Hand	HMV POP 222
LEE MARVIN		
220	Wand'rin' Star	Paramount PARA 3004
MASH		
278	Theme From M*A*S*H (Suicide Is Painless)	CBS 8536

Rank	Title	Label & No.

OLIVIA NEWTON-JOHN AND THE ELECTRIC LIGHT ORCHESTRA
402   Xanadu .... Jet 185
See also Olivia Newton-John, Electric Light Orchestra, John Travolta and Olivia Newton-John

NICOLE
450   A Little Peace .... CBS A 2365

NILSSON
53   Without You .... RCA 2165

1910 FRUITGUM CO.
869   Simon Says ...... Pye International 7N 25447

NU SHOOZ
873   I Can't Wait .... Atlantic A 9446

GARY NUMAN
121   Are 'Friends' Electric ....
.... Beggars Banquet BEG 18
482   Cars .... Beggars Banquet BEG 23
Are 'Friends' Electric credits Tubeway Army

O

BILLY OCEAN
145   When The Going Gets Tough The Tough Get Going .... Jive JIVE 114
752   Red Light Spells Danger ...... GTO GT 85
848   Love Really Hurts Without You GTO GT 52

DES O'CONNOR
521   I Pretend .... Columbia DB 8397

ODYSSEY
358   Use It Up And Wear It Out .. RCA PB 1962

ESTHER AND ABI OFARIM
223   Cinderella Rockefella .... Phillips BF 1640

ROY ORBISON
198   Oh Pretty Woman ...... London HLU 9919
331   It's Over .... London HLU 9882
337   Only The Lonely .... London HLU 9149
688   Dream Baby .... London HLU 9511

DONNY OSMOND
84   Puppy Love .... MGM 2006 104
179   Young Love .... MGM 2006 300
465   The Twelfth Of Never .... MGM 2006 199
See also Donny and Marie Osmond, Osmonds

DONNY AND MARIE OSMOND
912   I'm Leaving It (All) Up To You ....
.... MGM 2006 446
See also Donny Osmond, Marie Osmond, Osmonds

LITTLE JIMMY OSMOND
77   Long Haired Lover From Liverpool ....
.... MGM 2006 109

MARIE OSMOND
867   Paper Roses .... MGM 2006 315
See also Donny and Marie Osmond, Osmonds

Rank	Title	Label & No.

OSMONDS
289   Love Me For A Reason ... MGM 2006 458
604   Crazy Horses .... MGM 2006 142
653   Let Me In .... MGM 2006 321
See also Donny Osmond, Donny & Marie Osmond, Marie Osmond

GILBERT O'SULLIVAN
409   Clair .... MAM 84
438   Get Down .... MAM 96

JOHNNY OTIS SHOW
578   Ma He's Making Eyes At Me ....
.... Capitol CL 14794

OTTAWAN
613   D.I.S.C.O. .... Carrere CAR 161

OUR KID
976   You Just Might See Me Cry ....
.... Polydor 2058 729

OVERLANDERS
319   Michelle................. Pye 7N 17034

P

ELAINE PAIGE AND BARBARA DICKSON
109   I Know Him So Well........ RCA CHESS 3

PAPER LACE
234   Billy Don't Be A Hero ... Bus Stop BUS 1014

SIMON PARK
120   Eye Level .... Columbia DB 8946

RAY PARKER JR.
624   Ghostbusters .... Arista ARIST 580

FREDA PAYNE
42   Band Of Gold........... Invictus INV 502

PEPSI AND SHIRLIE
782   Heartache .... Polydor POSP 837

PET SHOP BOYS
143   Always On My Mind ... Parlophone R 6171
275   It's A Sin .... Parlophone R 6158
440   West End Girls .... Parlophone R 6115
See also Pet Shop Boys and Dusty Springfield

PET SHOP BOYS AND DUSTY SPRINGFIELD
759   What Have I Done To Deserve This ...
.... Parlophone R 6163
See also Pet Shop Boys, Dusty Springfield

PETER AND GORDON
422   A World Without Love . Columbia DB 7225
898   True Love Ways .... Columbia DB 7524

PETER, PAUL AND MARY
923   Leavin' On A Jet Plane ....
.... Warner Brothers WB 7340

PETERS AND LEE
454   Welcome Home .... Phillips 6006 307

PILOT
299   January .... EMI 2255